Inside
Soviet Military
Intelligence

By the same Author

THE LIBERATORS
INSIDE THE SOVIET ARMY

Inside
Soviet Military
Intelligence

VIKTOR SUVOROV

Macmillan Publishing Company
New York

Macmillan Publishing Company
866 Third Avenue, New York, N.Y. 10022

Library of Congress Cataloging in Publication Data
Suvorov, Viktor.
  Inside Soviet military intelligence.
  Includes index.
  1. Soviet Union. Glavnoe razvedyvatel'noe upravlenie.
2. Suvorov, Viktor. I. Title.
UB251.S65S88 1984   355.3′432′0947   84-7187
ISBN 0-02-615510-9

Macmillan books are available at special discounts
for bulk purchases for sales promotions, premiums, fund-raising,
or educational use. Special editions or book excerpts can also be
created to specification. For details, contact:

Special Sales Director
Macmillan Publishing Company
866 Third Avenue
New York, New York 10022

10 9 8 7 6 5 4 3 2 1

Printed in the United States of America

To the memory
of Oleg Vladimirovich
Penkovsky

Contents

Contents

Introduction

There is but one opinion as to which country in the world possesses the most powerful secret intelligence service. Without the slightest doubt that country is the Soviet Union, and the name of the monstrous secret organisation without precedent in the history of mankind is the KGB. But on the question as to which country possesses the second most powerful secret organisation, the opinions of specialists differ. Strange as it may seem, the country to which this organisation belongs is also the Soviet Union, and the organisation itself is called the Chief Intelligence Directorate of the General Staff.

This book was written in order to confirm this simple fact.

At first it was conceived as an instructional manual for a narrow circle of specialists. Subsequently it was revised by the author for a wider public. The revision was confined mainly to the excision of certain definitions and technical details which would be of little interest. Even after this, there remained in the book many details of a technical nature, which may sometimes make for difficult reading. But though I may apologise, there is nothing to be done. In order to understand a disease (and the desire to understand a disease implies a desire to fight against it), one must know its pathology as well as its symptoms.

*

For one of their very first chosen myths, the communists decided to record that the organs of enforcement of the new State were not created until the nineteenth of December 1917. This falsehood was circulated in order to prove that Soviet power, in the first forty-one days of its existence, could dispense with the mass executions so familiar to other revolutions. The falsehood is easily exposed. It is sufficient to look at the editions of the Bolshevist papers for those days which shook the world. The Organs and subsequent mass executions existed from the first hour, the first minute, the first infantile wail of this Soviet power. That first night, having announced to the world the birth of the most bloodthirsty dictatorship in its history, Lenin appointed its leaders. Among them was comrade A. I. Rikov, the head of the People's Commissariat for Internal Affairs which sounds less innocuous in its abbreviation, NKVD. Comrade Rikov was later shot, but not before he had managed to write into the history of the Organs certain bloody pages which the Soviet leadership would prefer to forget about. Fifteen men have been appointed to the post of Head of the Organs, of which three were hounded out of the Soviet government with ignominy. One died at his post. One was secretly destroyed by members of the Soviet government (as was later publicly admitted). Seven comrades were shot or hanged, and tortured with great refinement before their official punishment. We are not going to guess about the futures of three still living who have occupied the post. The fate of the deputy heads has been equally violent, even after the death of comrade Stalin.

The paradox of this endless bloody orgy would seem to be this. Why does the most powerful criminal organisation in the world so easily and freely give up its leaders to be torn to pieces? How is the Politburo able to deal with them so unceremoniously, clearly not experiencing the slightest fear before these seemingly all-powerful personalities and the organisations headed by them? How is it that the Politburo has practically no difficulties in displacing not only individual heads of State Security but in destroying whole flocks of the most influential State Security officers? Where lies the secret of this limitless power of the Politburo?

The answer is very simple. The method is an old one and has been used successfully for thousands of years. It boils down to the principle: 'divide and rule'. In the beginning, in order to rule, Lenin divided everything in Russia that was capable of being divided, and ever since the communists have continued faithfully to carry out the instructions of the great founder of the first proletarian state.

Each system of governing the State is duplicated and reduplicated. Soviet power itself is duplicated. If one visits any regional committee of the Party and then the Regional Executive Committee one is struck by the fact that two separate organisations having almost identical structures and deciding identical problems nevertheless take completely contradictory decisions. Neither one of these organisations has the authority to decide anything independently.

This same system exists at all stages and at all levels of the Government. If we look at the really important decisions of the Soviet leadership, those which are published in the papers, we will find that any one of them is taken only at joint sessions of the Central Committee of the Party and the Council of Ministers. I have in front of me as I write the last joint resolution on raising the quality and widening the range of production of children's toys. Neither the Council of Ministers of the gigantic State structure nor the Central Committee of the ruling Party is able, since neither has the power and authority, to take an independent decision on such an important matter. But we are not talking here just about Ministers and First Secretaries. At all lower levels the same procedure is to be observed. For example, only a joint decision of the Central Committee of the Communist Party of a republic and the Council of Ministers of the same republic, or the Provincial Committee and the Provincial Executive Committee, is valid. At these levels of course, such crucial problems as the quality of children's toys are not decided; but the principle remains that no separate and independent decisions can be taken. In shape and form, Soviet power is everywhere duplicated, from the planning of rocket launchings into space to the organisation for the burial of Soviet citizens, from the management of diplomatic missions abroad to lunatic asylums, from the construction of sewers to atomic ice-breakers.

In addition to the governing organs which give orders and see that they are carried out, there also exist Central Control Organs which are independent of the local authority. The basic one of these is of course the KGB, but independently of the KGB other powerful organs are also active: the innocent-sounding People's Control for example, a secret police organisation subordinated to a Politburo member who exercises almost as much influence as the Chief of the KGB. In addition to the People's Control, the Ministry of the Interior is also active and this is subordinated neither to the KGB nor to Control. There is also the Central Organ of the press, a visit of which to a factory or workshop causes hardly less anger than a visit of the OBHSS, the socialist fraud squad. On the initiative of Lenin, it was seen as essential that each powerful organ or organisation which is capable of taking independent decisions be counter-balanced by the existence of another no less powerful bureaucratic organisation. The thinking goes: we have a newspaper *Pravda*, let's have another on a similar scale – *Izvestia*. Tass created, as a counter-balance to it, APN. Not for competition but simply for duplication. In this way the comrades in the Politburo are able to live a quieter life. To control everybody and everything is absolutely impossible, and this is why duplication exists. Everybody jealously pursues his rival and in good time informs whoever he should inform of any flashes of inspiration, of any deviation from the established norm, any effort to look at what is going on from the standpoint of a healthy critical mind. Duplication in everything is the prime principle and reason behind the terrifying stagnation of all walks of life in Soviet society. It is also the reason for the unprecedented stability of the regime. In duplicating the Organs, the Politburo was able to neutralise any attempt by them to raise the standard of revolt against their creators, and thus it has always been.

The creation of a system of parallel institutions began with the creation of the Tcheka, an organisation called into existence to counter-balance the already growing powers of the People's Commissariat for Internal Affairs. During the course of the whole of the civil war these two bloody organisations existed independently, and as rivals, of each other. Their influence grew to immense proportions, and Lenin suggested the creation of yet another independent organ to carry out the task of control and retribution, the Rabkrin. This organ, known today as the People's Control, is still waiting for somebody to research into its history. The Rabkrin was Lenin's love-child, remembered by him even on his death-bed. The Rabkrin or, more formally, the Workers' and Peasants' Inspectorate was not created as an organ of repression for the whole population, but as an organisation for the control of the ruling Bolshevik élite and, above all, the Tcheka and the People's Commissariat for Internal Affairs.

In the meantime the tentacles of the Tcheka had spread out over the frontiers and the Bolkshevik leaders were forced to create yet another parallel organisation to the Tcheka, capable of counter-balancing its external activities. Neither the People's Commissariat nor the Rabkrin was able to fulfil this role. On the personal order of the indefatigable Lenin on 21 October 1918, an external intelligence service, completely independent of the Tcheka, was created under the meaningless title of the Registered Directorate of the Workers' and Peasants' Red Army. At the present time it is called the Chief Intelligence Directorate of the General Staff of the Soviet Army, and also known by its military classification as 'unit 44388'. In history there is a number of examples of similar organisations within repressive regimes. The most obvious of these is of course Hitler's Germany. The SS and the SA and, on the front, the Wehrmacht Divisions and the Divisions of the SS, all existed under the same duplication principle, as did the two Intelligence Services, the Gestapo and the Abwehr.

This multiplication of institutions can only be explained by the desire of the ruling class to guarantee the stability of its regime. It is important to clarify this, so that one can understand the role of Soviet military intelligence in Soviet society and in the international arena, and, in addition, the reason why this organisation has remained throughout Soviet history largely independent from the KGB, in spite of the many ordeals it has been subjected to.

Part One

Part One

Chapter One

The Triumvirate

The Party, the KGB and the Army form the triumvirate which rules the Soviet Union. All other institutions and organisations, including those which appear officially to wield State power, occupy a subordinate position. But no single one of the three holds absolute power. They are all interdependent and have to share power with their rivals. There is a constant underlying struggle between these three forces, with attacks and retreats, bloody skirmishes, victories, defeats, armistices, secret alliances and permanent treachery.

The Party cannot exist without a continuous repression of the people, in other words without the KGB. The KGB in turn cannot exist without a continuous fanning of the flames of communist fanaticism and the deception of the people, in other words without the Party. Each of the two considers its own function to be the important one and the function of its rival merely supplementary. Thus the Party and the KGB are striving for undivided rule, but with this in mind each understands that it is not possible to kill off its rival. Too much depends on the continued existence of that rival. Both the Party and the KGB need the Army, which plays the part of a performing crocodile, ensuring a quiet life for the other two. In the triumvirate system the Army is the most powerful element but it is also the most deprived as regards its rights. Unlike the Party and the KGB, the Army has never played the leading role in the trio. Should this ever happen, the Party and the KGB would be swiftly destroyed. The fact is that this crocodile does not need either the Party or the KGB. Its natural state is a free life in a swamp, enjoying the ability to gobble up whatever it wishes. Both the Party and the KGB are perfectly well aware that they, in the role of trainers of the performing crocodile, would be its first victims should the crocodile ever be set at liberty. So why has the crocodile never gobbled up its trainers?

The Party and the KGB hold the crocodile firmly in check by means of two strong leashes. The Party leash is called the Political Department, that of the KGB the Special Department. Every organ of the Army is penetrated by the Political Department of the Party and the Special Department of the KGB. On those occasions when the Army has attacked the Party, which has happened several times, beginning with the military opposition of the twenties, the Tchekists of the KGB have come into action and quickly gained control over dissident elements in the Army. When the Army has attacked the KGB, as happened after the death of Stalin, the Party has gone into action against it. And at times when the KGB has been plotting against the Party, the Party has invariably allowed the crocodile to take a bite at the Tchekists, but not a bite to the death. After such incidents the situation has returned to normal – the crocodile's trainers have manipulated their leashes in such a way and from different sides that it is impossible for any quarrel to have a conclusion. They have even been able to give the crocodile a few kicks and, if necessary, to direct it to another side, as it is said 'against any aggressor'. Its dependent situation notwith-standing, the Army is sufficiently strong sometimes to pull its two trainers after it. Thus it is not possible for the Army to be left out of the triumvirate. None of the remaining inhabitants of the Soviet Union has any independent part to play in the concert. They fulfil an auxiliary role. They supply food to the trainers and the croco-dile, put on their make-up for the show, announce the different acts and collect money from the terrified spectators.

The general staff of the Soviet Army is the brain of the crocodile, and military intelligence is its eyes and ears. The GRU is a part of the general staff, in other words a part of the brain. In fact it is that part which analyses what the eyes see and the ears hear, the part which concentrates the unblinking eyes of the crocodile onto the most interesting targets and trains its ears to hear with precision every rustle of the night. Although the crocodile is firmly tied to the Party and the KGB, the general staff and the integral GRU are practically independent of external control. Why this should be is explained by the Party's experience. In the period before the war, the Party supervised the general staff so carefully, and the Tchekists insisted strongly on the observance of every minute directive of the Party, that the general staff completely lost the ability to think independently. As a result the crocodile, despite its enormous size, completely lost its presence of mind, its speed of reaction and any capability to think and take independent decisions. All this brought the system to the edge of catastrophe, as the Army became practically incapable of fighting. The Party learnt from this sad experience and realised that it must not interfere in the working of the crocodile's brain, even if this brain had ceased to think along Party lines. The Party and the KGB preferred, for purely practical reasons, to keep only the body of the crocodile under control and not to interfere with the work of its brain, of its sharp ears and piercing eyes.

Chapter Two

History

Soviet military intelligence* and its superior organ, the GRU, are an integral part of the Army. The history of Soviet intelligence can therefore only be surveyed in the light of the history of the development of the Army and consequently in the light of the continuous struggle between the Army, the Party and the KGB.

From the moment of the creation of the first detachment of the Red Army, small intelligence groups were formed within these detachments quietly and often without any order from above. As the regular army developed into newly-formed regiments, brigades, divisions, army corps and armies, so these intelligence organs developed with it. From the outset, intelligence units at all levels were subordinated to the corresponding staffs. At the same time the superior echelons of intelligence exercised control and direction of the lower echelons. The chief of intelligence of an army corps, for example, had his own personal intelligence unit and in addition directed the chiefs of intelligence of the divisions which formed a part of his army corps. Each divisional intelligence chief, in his turn, had *his* own intelligence unit at the same time as directing the activities of the intelligence chiefs of the brigades which formed his division. And so on down the scale. On 13 June 1918 a front was formed, for the first time in the composition of the Red Army. This front received the name of the Eastern Front, and in it there were five armies and the Volga military flotilla. On the same day there was created a 'registrational' (intelligence) department in the Eastern Front. The department had the intelligence chiefs of all five armies and the flotilla

* The Russian version of the English 'intelligence' – razvedka – has wider significance and includes everything we understand by the terms 'intelligence', 'reconnaissance', 'surveillance' and all activity governing collection and processing of information about actual or potential enemies.

6

reporting to it. These intelligence chiefs of the front possessed a number of aircraft for aerial reconnaissance, some cavalry squadrons and, most important, an agent network. The agent network for the Eastern Front was first formed on the basis of underground organisations of Bolsheviks and other parties which supported them. Subsequently the network grew and, during the advances of the Eastern Front in the Urals and in Siberia, agent groups and organisations intervened in the rear of the enemy before the main forces attacked. Subsequent to the formation of the Eastern Front, new fronts were added to the Red Army: the Southern, Ukrainian, Northern, Turkistan and, later, Caucasian, Western, South-Eastern, North-Eastern and others. The intelligence set-up for each front was organised in the same way as that for the Eastern Front. There were also some independent and separate armies which did not form part of the fronts, and these, as a rule, had their own independent networks.

In the spring of 1918, besides the agent, aerial and other types of intelligence services, the diversionary intelligence service came into being. These diversionary detachments reported to the intelligence chiefs of fronts, armies, corps and sometimes divisions, and were called the 'cavalry of special assignments'. Formed from the best cavalrymen in the Army, they dressed in the uniform of the enemy and were used to carry out deep raids in the enemy's rear, to take prisoners – especially staff officers – to collect information on enemy positions and activities and to undermine and sometimes physically destroy the enemy's command structure. The number of these diversionary units and their numerical strength constantly increased. In 1920, on the Polish Front, on the staff of the Soviet forces, there was a separate cavalry brigade for 'special assignments' with a strength of more than two thousand cavalrymen, and this was on top of several regiments and separate squadrons. All these units were dressed in Polish uniform. Much later these diversionary units received the name Spetsnaz, now given to all special forces of the GRU.

From its inception, military intelligence suffered the greatest possible antagonism from the Tchekists. The Tcheka had its own central agent network and an agent network in local areas. The Tchekists jealously guarded their right to have secret agents and could not resign themselves to the idea that anyone else was operating similar secret networks. The Tcheka also had units of

7

'special assignments' which carried out raids, not in the enemy's rear, but in its own rear, destroying those who were dissatisfied with the communist order.

During the civil war the Tcheka strove to unite all special assignment units under its own control. Several cases are recorded of the Tchekists trying to take over organs of military intelligence. One such attempt occurred on 10 July 1918 when the Tcheka shot the whole staff of the Eastern Front intelligence department, which had been in existence for only twenty-seven days, together with the entire staff of the front and the commander himself, M. A. Muravev, who had been trying to intervene in favour of his intelligence department. The whole of the agent system of military intelligence passed into the control of the Tchekists, but this brought the front to the very edge of catastrophe. The new commander, I. I. Vatsetis, and his chief of staff had no intelligence service of their own, and were unable to ask for the necessary information. They could only request information in a very tactful way, being well aware of the Tcheka's attitude to those it disliked. (As regards Vatsetis the Tchekists did indeed shoot him, but much later.)

Naturally while the agent network was under the control of the Tcheka, its own work was given priority, and any tasks set it by the Army Command were given very low priority. This of course brought the forces very near to complete defeat. If the army intelligence service is separated from the army staff, then the brain becomes nothing more than the brain of a blind and deaf man. Even if the blind man receives essential information from one source or another, his reaction will still be slow and his movements imprecise. The leader of the Red Army, Trotsky, placed an ultimatum before Lenin: either give me an independent military intelligence service or let Dzerzhinsky lead the Army with his Tchekists.

Lenin knew what the Tcheka was capable of but he also knew that its capabilities were extremely one-sided. He therefore ordered Dzerzhinsky not to interfere in matters of military intelligence. In spite of this, the Tcheka's attempts to swallow up military intelligence went on, and these efforts still continue on a reduced scale up to the present day.

Towards the end of 1918 the organisation of military intelligence from regimental staff level up to the level of front staff had been virtually completed. There remained only one staff which was deprived of its own intelligence service of the Republic, the staff of the Red Army (at that time called the Field Staff, later the General Staff). For this reason the general staff remained blind and deaf, obtaining information indispensable to its work at second- or third-hand. In addition to this, the absence of a superior intelligence organ meant a complete lack of co-ordination of the front intelligence services. Military intelligence had acquired a pyramid structure, but the top of the pyramid was missing. The Chief of the Army and in charge of all military production, Leon Trotsky several times approached Lenin with the demand that he should create such a superior military intelligence organ. Understanding the necessity for the creation of such an organ, but realising that this would inevitably mean a strengthening of the position of Trotsky, Lenin prevaricated and repeatedly refused Trotsky's suggestion. At the beginning of autumn, the position of the communists worsened sharply. Production, fuel and political crises became more acute. Armed uprisings were taking place against the communists. There was an attempt on the life of Lenin himself. In order to save the regime the communists decided on a desperate measure. In each town and village they would take hostages and, in the case of the slightest manifestation of discontent among the inhabitants, these hostages would be shot. The Soviet state was saved, by mass executions. Then another problem arose. The Tcheka, released from its restraints and drunk with blood, got out of control. In Tver and Torzhok the Tchekists, together with the hostages, destroyed communist leaders who displeased them. One threat to the stability of the state had been replaced by another, far worse. Lenin, not yet completely recovered, immediately resumed day-to-day leadership. Without restricting the terror, he took a number of steps to control it. The most important of his decisions were, firstly, to give to the People's Commissariats (i.e. the ministries), the provincial and town committees the right to take part in court cases against arrested communists. A communist would be declared not guilty if two members of the Party Committee testified in his favour. Secondly, Lenin directed his attention to the annulment of the Tcheka's monopoly of secret activity. He finally accepted Trotsky's proposal and on 21 October 1918 signed a decree, creating a superior organ of Soviet military intelligence which was to be called the Registrational Directorate of the Field Staff of the Republic.

The newly created directorate did not increase or decrease the importance of the front and army intelligence services, it merely co-ordinated them. But at this time the directorate began the creation of a new network of agents which could be active in countries all over the world, including those where the front networks already had active agents. The organisation created in 1918 has, in principle, survived to the present day. Certainly the founding rules are fully applicable to our own time. These are, firstly, that each military staff must have its own independent intelligence set-up. Secondly, the intelligence set-up of sub-ordinate staffs is to be fully under the command of the intelligence of superior formations. Thirdly, the agent network must be part of the composition of the general staff intelligence network *and* part of the composition of the front and fleet intelligence services. (In peace-time this means military districts and groups of forces.) Fourthly, diversionary intelligence is subsidiary to agent intelligence. It must be found on front or fleet level, military districts and groups of forces and also at the level of armies and flotillas. And, fifthly and most importantly, military intelligence must be quite separate from the organs of enforcement and their intelligence services. Since 1918, each one of these rules has been broken at least once, if not more often, but invariably the mistake has been summarily corrected.

The creation of the GRU* was not only an act of self-preservation on Lenin's part from the ravages of the Tcheka, but also a concession to Trotsky. Having entrusted this weapon to Trotsky and the Army, Lenin was careful to equip it with a safety device by the name of Simon Ivanovich Aralov, who came from the V. Tcheka. On becoming chief of the registrational directorate, Aralov formally remained a member of the collegium of the Tcheka. This step was taken in the interests of subterfuge, and even up to the present day has confused many researchers. Remaining formally within the Tcheka, Aralov, from the first day of his work in military intelligence, had to become a rival and consequently enemy of the Tchekists. This had entered into

* The GRU, like the KGB, has been through several name changes in its history; at this time it was called 'Registraupr', later 'Razvedupr'. For our present purposes the name GRU will be used consistently.

Lenin's calculations; he had not been slow to see that it would be impossible for Aralov to avoid daily skirmishes with the Tchekists on the most mundane questions, and that this would inevitably lead to a confrontation which would preclude any possibility of Aralov being exploited as a trusted Tchekist. But this was not all. In the case of any agreement with the Army, not one of the Army's chiefs would dare to trust Aralov. The GRU would be a part of the Army but the Army would not be able to make use of the GRU in the struggle against the Party and the Tcheka.

Lenin's calculations proved themselves sound remarkably quickly. In the spring of 1919 the reinforced army under Trotsky's leadership openly came out against the Party's meddling in the affairs of the Army. A united group of Army delegates, the so-called 'Military Opposition', at the eighth congress of the Party in March 1919, demanded *de facto* independence of the Army from Party influences. At that time it was still permitted to express personal opinions at party conferences, and more than 100 delegates out of 269 declared themselves in favour of the military programme. There were widespread abstentions and the Party and the Tcheka found themselves in a minority at their own conference.

Only a few votes were necessary to secure the complete and legal victory of the Army, but at this point the delegates from the military intelligence service, knowing the heavy hand of Aralov, maintained an icy silence and strict neutrality. Then at the most dramatic moment of the session Aralov spoke critically of the military opposition, after which the delegates of the military intelligence service with one voice supported the Party. The number of supporters of the military opposition shrank to ninety-five, a clear defeat. The session closed with a victory for the Party. The military opposition crumbled and many of its members never again took any action against the Party. The Army had learnt a lesson. In the struggle against the Party, never count on the support of the military intelligence service. Emboldened by victory, the Tcheka renewed its penetration of the Army. Many unrepentant members of the military opposition were arrested and shot. The humiliation of the Army inevitably affected military intelligence too, and on 13 May 1919 the Tchekists executed members of the staff of military intelligence in the 7th Army who had displeased them. Military intelligence naturally objected sharply to the Tcheka's taking the law into its own hands, and from that time on it was its sworn enemy. Lenin was delighted. Military intelligence henceforth was an inseparable part of the Army, but its chief was the personal enemy of both the Army and the Tcheka. Another unwritten rule was established in the organisation of the GRU, too, which was that the chief of the GRU must be appointed only from among the senior officials of the Tcheka secret police (historically known as the V. Tcheka, GPU, OGPU, NKVD, NKGB, MGB, MVD and KGB and unofficially as 'the Organs'). This rule has also been broken several times, but the Party has always been able to correct its mistake in time.

The agent network of the GRU was reinforced at almost lightning speed. There are several reasons for this. Firstly, inside Russia after the Revolution, in her central provinces alone, there were more than four million foreigners: Germans, Austrians, Hungarians, Poles, Slovaks, Czechs, Koreans, Bulgars, Serbs, Croats and others. Most of them were former prisoners of war. More than three hundred thousand of them voluntarily enlisted in the Red Army. There was no need to recruit such people. The overwhelming majority of them were convinced, fanatical communists. Military intelligence simply sent them off to their own countries as GRU agents. Secondly, after the Revolution Moscow became the Mecca of communism, and after the foundation of the Comintern, communists from all countries flocked to Moscow. The Comintern openly declared as its aim the destruction of capitalism, and in this manifesto it was helped from all sides, the Tcheka and the GRU in particular developing their espionage activities. On the orders of the Comintern,* thousands of communists spread into foreign states worldwide under the control of the Soviet intelligence organisations. Some of these, like the German communists Richard Sorge and Karl Ramm, the Finnish communist Otto Kusinien, the Hungarian Sandor Rado, are now well known to history, but thousands more remained unknown, activists labouring strenuously to fulfil the will of Soviet intelligence. Thirdly, after the Revolution millions of émigrés appeared from Russia, all over the world. Any Soviet intelligence officer

* The Communist International, grouping together the communist parties of the world and declaring itself as 'the headquarters of the worldwide communist revolution'.

who had undergone the most elementary linguistic training could move about freely from country to country without attracting the slightest suspicion.

External circumstances favoured communism too. After the First World War the world veered sharply towards communist doctrines. Communist parties were strong and united. In Germany and Hungary there were communist revolutions. The heat of the conflagration was felt in Spain, France and China. Soviet intelligence skilfully exploited the situation which was unfolding. The First World War also left behind a legacy of despair – the world had given way and there were many people who had lost their hopes and ideals. Embittered and depressed, their recruitment presented no difficulty whatsoever. In one of the early GRU instruction manuals there is the following advice: 'If you need a facilities agent (a radio operator, owner of a safe house or transmission point) find a tall handsome man who has lost a leg or an arm in the war.'

One last, but by no means negligible factor, is that Russia has always possessed too much gold. After the Revolution, mountains of gold from millions of people killed in the torture chambers of Soviet power were added to the State Treasury. In addition to this, communists plundered churches all over Russia which from ancient times had been famous for their wealth. Great profit was harvested from the domes of the richest cathedrals, for these were roofed with solid gold. In looting the churches, the communists said, 'For the needs of the world revolution.' What they meant was, 'For the needs of espionage.'

*

There were many elementary errors and failures in the work of these early field officers who had no experience whatsoever. For example, the counter-intelligence officers of Lithuania, Latvia and Estonia, which at the time were independent states, simply told any suspicious person who claimed to be a fugitive Russian officer, or engineer or doctor, to tie a necktie. In 1920, by this method alone, more than forty GRU agents were unmasked in these three small countries. The GRU was unperturbed by these failures, however, its philosophy being that if it could not have quality it would go for quantity. It was an astute calculation. If one agent in a hundred sent abroad showed himself to be talented, and his natural talent made up for his lack of education, then that was enough. Nobody was worried about the agents who were discovered. Let them get out of the mess if they could. The Soviet Union will never admit that the people it sends out belong to Soviet intelligence.

This large-scale attack was highly successful. Out of the thousands of intelligence agents sent abroad, some dozen began to give positive results. The help of communists abroad also began to tell. Gradually quality began to creep into the work of the GRU. One of the first outstanding successes was the creation of the so-called 'Mrachkovski Enterprises' or, as it was officially called in GRU documents, 'the network of commercial undertakings'. Jacob Mrachkovski (his brother was a member of the Central Committee) was sent to Germany where he organised a small shop and then a small factory. Subsequently he bought, in fictitious names, several factories in France, Great Britain, Canada, the United States and finally China. The money put into these undertakings quickly grew and, after several years, the Mrachovski undertakings began to show profits of tens of millions of pounds. The money earned was used by the GRU as its chief source of 'clean' money, that is, money which had never been on Soviet territory and consequently could be used for agents' operations. In addition to obtaining money the Mrachkovski undertakings were widely used for the legalisation of newly posted intelligence officers who by now were beginning to be better trained. Journeying from country to country, they found help and support from the Mrachkovski network. They got themselves jobs and after some months received the most laudatory references and went off into other countries where the same thing took place. This went on until the agent was able to stand on his own two feet. The security of the network was so tight that no undertaking ever suspected the existence of another. Mrachkovski himself travelled all over the world, buying up new enterprises, installing one or two of his own people and obtaining perfectly legal and highly lucrative licences and patents.

Relations with the Tchekists were gradually stretched to their limit. The Party was striving to inflame the hostility between the GRU and the Organs of State. Lenin made a great success of this, as did his successors. The next conflict broke out in the spring of 1920. Both Lenin and Trotsky considered themselves outstanding

14

thinkers, theoreticians and practical men; men of deep knowledge as regards military affairs and international relations. Naturally neither one nor the other took any notice of evaluated intelligence. They both demanded that the intelligence material should be laid before them 'grey' and unevaluated: they would then draw their own conclusions and analyse the material on the basis of Marxist doctrine. But Marxism had very precisely and categorically foretold that there would be a world war in Europe which would be the last war of mankind. The imperialist war would develop into a worldwide revolution, after which a golden age would begin. Yet the war had finished two years before and no worldwide revolution had happened. Intelligence reported that there were no signs of this revolution coming about, so both Lenin and Trotsky were either compelled to admit that Marxism was wrong or to take measures to bring the revolution about. They decided to trigger off a revolution in Europe, starting with Poland. Intelligence assessments were ignored, and naturally the adventure ended in complete failure. Both the organisers immediately started to hunt for a scapegoat. The only possible explanation for the scandal was that the intelligence service had done its work badly. Lenin announced to the rank and file of the Party, 'We have suffered this defeat as a result of the negligence of the intelligence service.' But the GRU was a completely unknown entity, even to some of the highest representatives of the Soviet bureaucracy, and much more so to the rank-and-file Party members. All eyes turned towards the Tchekists. Their unpopularity among the people, even before this, was evident. After Lenin's announcement their authority finally fell. Dzerzhinsky caused a scandal in the Kremlin and demanded explanations from the Politburo. In order to calm the Tchekists and to support his own version of the story, Lenin permitted the Tchekists to purge the GRU. The first bloody purge took place in November 1920. On Lenin's orders hundreds of intelligence officers who had allegedly failed to evaluate the situation correctly were shot.

Up to this time there had been no need to account for the GRU's activities, but now information was made available to some Party members. This has led some specialists to the mistaken conclusion that the GRU did not exist until this time.

However, the GRU did not take long to recover from the 1920 purge. This may be explained mainly by the fact that the overseas organs of the GRU were practically untouched, and this for eminently sound reasons. Neither Lenin nor Trotsky had any idea of shooting the intelligence officers who were overseas, not only because they were manifestly innocent, but also because their deaths would have absolutely no salutary effect on others since nobody would hear about them, not even the many members of the Central Committee. The other reason for the quick recovery of the GRU was that its agent intelligence network in the military districts was also left untouched. At the end of the civil war, the fronts were tranformed into 'military districts', but the chain of command in the new districts did not undergo any essential changes. A 'registration' department was included on the strength of the staff of each district which continued in peace-time to carry on agent intelligence work in countries where the district would have to carry out military activities in any future war. Up to the time of the 1920 purge there were fifteen military districts and two fleets in the Red Army. They all carried out, independently from each other, agent intelligence work of a very intensive nature.

The internal military districts were no exception. Their intelligence centres were moved out to the frontiers and it was from there that the direction of agents was undertaken. Each internal military district also has its tasks in wartime, and its intelligence work is based around these tasks. The direction of activities of a frontier district is very precisely defined; at the same time the internal district, independent of circumstances, may operate in different directions. Consequently its agent network in peace-time operates in different directions, too. For example, in 1920 agents of the Moscow military district operated on the territories of Poland, Lithuania (at that time still independent) and Finland. This system has prevailed in all respects, except that the districts and fleets have become more numerous, as also has money available for intelligence. We are richer now than we were then.

*

After 1927 Soviet military intelligence began to blossom. This was the year in which the first five-year plan was drawn up, which aimed (as all subsequent five-year plans have) exclusively at the growth of the military potential of the country. The plan stipulated the creation and speedy growth of the tank, ship-building, aviation and artillery industries. The Soviet Union set itself the target of creating the most powerful army in the world. The Soviet leadership made haste and demanded from its designers not only the creation of new kinds of weaponry and military technology, but also that Soviet armaments must be the best in the world. Monumental sums of money were spent to attain this aim: practically the whole of Russia's gold reserves was thrown into the task. At Western auctions the Soviet authorities sold off Russian corn and wood, pictures by Rembrandt and Nicholas II's stamp collection. A tidy sum of money was realised.

All GRU residents received book-length lists of foreign military technology which they would have to steal in the near future. The lists included equipment for bombers and fighters, anti-aircraft and anti-tank guns, howitzers and mortars, submarines and torpedo boats, radio valves and tank engines, the technology for the production of aluminium and equipment for boring out gun barrels. Yet another GRU tradition first saw the light of day in this period: that of stealing analogous kinds of armaments at the same time in different countries and then studying them to select the best. Thus, at the beginning of the 1930s, Soviet military intelligence succeeded in stealing samples or plans of torpedoes in Italy, France, the United States, Germany and Great Britain. It was hardly surprising that the Soviet torpedo, manufactured in the shortest possible time, conformed to the highest international standards. Sometimes Soviet copiers selected the best assemblies and components and constructed out of them a new type which often turned out to be the very best in the world. Luck too was on the side of Soviet military intelligence. Nobody took very seriously the efforts of the Soviet Union in the military sphere, and few countries went to great pains to hide their secrets from it. Communists the world over were obsessed by the idea of helping Soviet intelligence, Soviet residents were able to throw their money round, and finally the great depression threw into the arms of Soviet intelligence thousands of opportunists who feared losing their factories, workshops or offices. Soviet intelligence, by the beginning of the 1930s, had attained unprecedented heights of power. Within Soviet territory the GRU had practically no political influence. In the international sphere it did not very much seek to enter into the political life of parties and states, but in the field of clean espionage the GRU already clearly occupied the leading position in the world, having by far overtaken the political intelligence work of the OGPU. At the beginning of the 1930s the GRU budget was several times larger than the overseas budget of the OGPU. This situation remains true today.

The system in use today of recruitment and running of agents had already fully developed by the end of the 1920s. In agent organisations directly subordinated to the GRU the recruitment and running of agents was in the hands of 'illegals', that is, GRU officers posted abroad undercover with forged documents and offices, posing as Soviet diplomats, consuls, trade representatives, correspondents and so on. In agent organisations subordinated to military districts and fleets the recruitments of agents was carried out from the territory of the Soviet Union. Only rarely did certain officers of the intelligence directorates of districts travel abroad with forged documents for short periods. Before diplomatic recognition of the Soviet Union, emphasis was concentrated on the activities of illegals, but after its recognition, undercover residencies were added to the numerous illegal residencies. The GRU illegals and undercover residencies acted independently from each other but in the pre-war period the communications of illegals from GRU residencies with the Centre were frequently accomplished through the Soviet embassies. This was a very serious mistake. With the beginning of the war when the embassies were closed or blockaded, the communication with illegals was disrupted. The mistake was subsequently rectified. Military district intelligence always operated independently of the GRU illegals and Soviet embassies, and for this reason at the beginning of the war it was practically unharmed. Gradually a tendency became noticeable in the operations of military district intelligence services to limit the use of Soviet officers even for short trips abroad. Faced with wartime conditions the military district intelligence services began to recruit and run their agents only from Soviet territory. The recruitment of new agents was carried out either on Soviet territory or on the territory of neighbouring countries by means of agents who had been recruited earlier.

There is an interesting story to be told about the recruitment of agents at this time, whose moral holds as true today. In the pre-war period, recruitment took up little time. The Comintern simply made a decision and immediately scores, sometimes hundreds of communists became Soviet secret agents. In the

18

interests of successful agent work, the GRU always demanded from them that they should publicly resign from the communist party. The vast majority accepted this without demur. After all, it was only a camouflage, a Bolshevik manoeuvre to help defeat the class enemy. Sometimes however, there were communists who were unwilling. In Germany, one group agreed to the GRU's demands only on condition that it was accepted into the Communist Party of the Soviet Union. The demand was a simple one, for it is not difficult for the GRU to write out a dozen new party cards, and as the new agent group was working so successfully, the GRU did not want to refuse. At a routine meeting the GRU case officer, an employee of the Soviet embassy in Berlin, informed the group's leader that their demands had been met. He congratulated the group on becoming members of the CPSU and informed them, in conclusion, that the General Secretary of the Party himself, comrade Stalin, had written out the party cards. As an exceptional case, the German communists had been accepted without going through the candidacy stage. Their party cards were naturally to be kept in the Central Committee.

At this news the group's productivity redoubled. It was supposed to receive a certain sum of money for its work, but the group members refused to accept the money. More than that, they began to hand over to their case officers sums of their own money, in order to pay their membership fees to the Soviet communist party. Punctually they handed over to their case officers all documents and payslips concerning their earnings together with their party subscriptions. This took up a great deal of time during the agent meetings, but the Germans were working very productively and nobody wanted to offend them.

Some time later, the Gestapo got on their trail, but all the members of the group managed to escape into Austria, then to Switzerland and finally through France to Spain where the civil war was going on. From Spain they were brought to Moscow. Terrible disappointments awaited them in the capital of the proletariat of all the world, the chief of which was that nobody had at any time written out their party cards, or accepted them into the Soviet communist party. The GRU officials had of course assumed that the agents would never set foot in the Soviet Union and that therefore it would be very easy to dupe them. However, on their arrival in Moscow, the first thing the agents did was to declare a hunger strike and demand a meeting with the higher leadership of the GRU. The meeting took place and the GRU leadership did all in its power to help the Germans join the party, after going through the candidate stage, naturally. But foreigners can only be accepted in the CPSU through the Central Committee, and the natural questions arose: 'Were you ever members of the communist party? Why did you leave it?' The fanatics told exactly what had really happened but were damned out of their own mouths. To burn one's party card is a cardinal sin – and the Central Committee threw out their application. The Germans again declared a hunger strike and demanded a meeting with Stalin in person. At this point the NKVD offered its help to the Central Committee, but the GRU intervened, being in no way desirous that its agents should fall into the hands of the NKVD. So the ex-agents ended up in the GRU cellars.

In the meantime, the political situation had changed sharply. Hitler had become Stalin's best friend and the communists likewise friends of the fascists. There ensued an exchange of gifts – the most up-to-date German military aeroplanes for Stalin (including the top secret ME109, JU87, JU88, DO217, HE111 and even the ME110) in exchange for the surrender of all German communists who had taken political asylum in the Soviet Union. Hitler's calculation was very simple. In the short time before war broke out, the Russians would not be able to copy the planes, but he would have the heads of his political opponents. It was a fruitful deal for Stalin too. He was bored with the German communists and now he would be able to give them to the Gestapo in exchange for the best German aeroplanes. In addition to the ordinary members, there were members of the German Central Committee and the Politburo, together with the editors of the communist newspaper. These were not taken to Germany, but the Gestapo was told it could shoot them in situ, in the Moscow area. However, as far as the former GRU agents were concerned, the decision had been taken not to hand them over. They knew too much. The German embassy in Moscow was informed that they had all died in Spain and had never got as far as Moscow. The fascists did not object but suggested they would present one more aircraft at the same price. Unfortunately, the former agents, not knowing anything about the bargaining that was going on, again declared a hunger strike, and this decided their fate. The Soviet side now admitted to the fascists that they were in Moscow and proposed a compromise. The fascists could shoot their victims in the Soviet Union without talking to them. The execution took place among the huge coal bunkers of the Kashierski Electric Power Station. Beforehand, the Gestapo men had personally identified each of the people to be executed and photographed them; then, under cover of protracted whistling of locomotives, they shot them all. Afterwards, joint detachments of the GRU, the Central Committee of the Soviet communist party and the Gestapo burnt the bodies in the furnaces of the power station.

The Germans' mistake was threefold: they believed too quickly in the promises of the GRU; they insisted too strongly on the GRU's fulfilling its promises; and they forgot that if somebody puts a high enough price on the head of an agent, however good he may be, the GRU will sell him without hesitation.

*

In the meantime the Party, under the leadership of Stalin, arrived face to face with the ultimate necessity of subjugating all layers of Soviet society and utterly eradicating dissension. The decision was taken by the Party to purge the whole country of potential dissidents. Today we have irrefutable proof that the 'Great Terror' was carefully planned and prepared. On the testimony of A. Avtorhanov the Central Committee of the Party had, as long ago as 13 May 1935, taken the decision to create a special security commission for carrying out mass repressions in the country, which took place in 1937 to 1938.

For almost two years the Special Commission prepared the most bloody page in the history of mankind. Its members were Stalin, Zhdanov, Yezhov, Shkiriatov, Malenkov and Voyshinski. It is interesting to note that the then head of NKVD, Yagoda, was not a member of the Commission, and this was a sensible move. Before carrying out its massive blood-letting of the whole of society, the Party took pains to purge the surgical instrument itself, the NKVD organs. The purge began secretly as early as 1935 and at that stage concerned only the organs and the overseas residencies of the NKVD. In order not to frighten anybody, it was carried out secretly and without public trials. Naturally it was the GRU which was entrusted with the task of purging the NKVD overseas organs. In 1935 Yan Karlovich Berzin, the GRU's chief, travelled to the Far East with special powers and a group of trusted helpers. Secret orders appointing one I. S. Unshlikht and later S. T. Uritski as chief of the GRU were issued. But no order was issued for Berzin to relinquish his post. In other words, the appointment of Uritski was simply a cover-up for the long absence of Berzin. In the Far East Berzin and his assistants secretly liquidated the leading illegals of the NKVD. In the following year Berzin, with his assistants, appeared in Spain. His official job was Chief Advisor to the Spanish Government, a post in which he was extremely active. Firstly, he endeavoured to direct the activities of the Spanish Government along lines favourable to Moscow. Secondly, he personally ran from Spain the whole of the overseas network of the GRU. And finally, he did not forget his most important task. The head of the Foreign Directorate of the NKVD, Slutski, was also in Spain, also personally supervising the activities of all his overseas agents. In all probability Slutski was aware that Berzin and the GRU had some connection with the mysterious disappearance of NKVD illegals. Evidence has been preserved which shows that Slutski and Berzin had clashes practically every day in Spain. However, at the same time, the intelligence chief of the NKVD was finding himself increasingly subject to the chief of Soviet military intelligence. At the end of September 1936 the NKVD chief, Yagoda, was dismissed from his post and the secretary of the Central Committee of the Party, Ezhov, was appointed in his place. Ezhov himself began a most cruel purge of the NKVD – and he no longer required the assistance of the GRU. More than 3,000 Tchekists were shot on Ezhov's orders, including Yagoda and Slutski themselves. It is interesting to note that Yagoda's death followed an open trial, but Slutski was murdered secretly, in the same way as his best illegal residents had been executed previously. After the Party, in the person of Ezhov and with the help of the GRU, had purged the NKVD, the time came for the Army to be dealt with. This purge began with the liquidation of the general staff – and the complete destruction of the GRU. Among those military leaders first executed together with Marshal Tukhachevski were army commanders Yakir and Uboreevich and Corps Commander Putna, the Soviet military attaché in London. As might be expected, all military attachés are GRU officers; but Putna was not simply a military attaché. Until his appointment to London he had been deputy chief of the GRU.

His execution served as an extra excuse for the NKVD to carry out a special purge in the ranks of the GRU. Hatred which had been collecting for many years at last came out into the open. In the course of the purge first the acting head of the GRU, Uritski, was arrested and shot, and after him all the rest. The NKVD and GRU now exchanged roles. NKVD men with special powers went around the world destroying both GRU illegals and also those intelligence officers of the GRU and NKVD who had refused to return to the Soviet Union and certain destruction. In the course of the 1937 purge the GRU was completely destroyed – even down to the lavatory attendants and cooks on its payroll. Berzin, back from Spain, had to re-create the GRU from scratch.

*

By the autumn of 1937, by a special effort of the Comintern – particularly in Spain with the help and coercion of the International Brigades – the GRU had somewhat recovered its strength. A year later Soviet military intelligence had returned to its stormy activities. But in the summer of 1938, in the course of a second wave of terror, the GRU was again destroyed, losing its entire strength. This time Berzin himself, one of the cleverest and most successful leaders the GRU has had, was among the victims.

The blow delivered automatically meant a blow to all organisations subordinate to the GRU, that is to the intelligence directorates of the military districts. Here the death-dealing whirlwind came twice, literally destroying everything. During the pre-war years, in the areas of western military districts the intelligence directorates had extended the existing reserves of underground armies in case of the occupation of these areas by an enemy. Secret depots and stores of weapons and explosives had been established, radio sets had been secreted and refuges for partisans and intelligence officers had been set up. In the terror, all this was destroyed, and tens of thousands of trained partisans and saboteurs, ready to meet the enemy, were shot or perished in prisons and concentration camps. Military intelligence ceased to exist. And not only military intelligence; the Army had been bled white, and military industry, too. But Ezhov, the head of the NKVD, had made a fatal mistake in taking Berzin's place when he was executed on 29 July 1938. The very next day, Stalin received only one report on both GRU and NKVD activities, instead of the usual two. The implication was clear: a monopoly of secret activity had begun, and Stalin now had no way to balance the power of the NKVD. With his customary precision and deliberation he realised that his control of Soviet intelligence was slipping away and the same day, 30 July, he set in train the events which would lead to Ezhov's removal and execution.

In the winter of 1939/40 there occurred an improbable scandal. The Red Army, whose strength at the moment of the attack was more than four million men, was unable to crush the resistance of the Finnish Army, whose strength was only 27,000 men. Reasons for this were quickly found. Of course there was the cold. (The German Army's right to claim the same reason for its defeat in the winter of 1941 was unanimously denied.) The second reason was the intelligence service. In all Soviet historical works (which may be published only with the permission of the Propaganda Department of the Party Central Committee), even to this day, the cold and poor intelligence are the reasons always given. The Party forgets to specify that from 1937 to 1939 Soviet military intelligence was practically non-existent, at the Party's own wish.

After the Finnish scandal, Stalin did not order a purge of the GRU. It is probable that at that time there was nobody to purge, but he still ordered the execution of General Proskurov, the new head of the GRU, and his staff because of Proskurov's disagreement with him over the Hitler-Stalin pact. In June 1940 General Filipp Golikov was appointed chief of the GRU. Under Golikov the GRU was reborn amazingly quickly into an effective intelligence force. There has been much speculation about this period. Did the GRU know of the plans for Germany's attack on the Soviet Union or not? The best answer to the question must lie in Golikov's own survival. Seven leaders before him and two after him were murdered, yet he went on to become Stalin's Deputy of Personnel and Marshal of the Soviet Union. The political leadership may not take the right decision, even with the best information that Golikov could give, but it will not bite the hand that feeds it.

The war had begun with a catastrophic defeat for the Soviet Union. In the first few hours the German Army succeeded in securing a strategic initiative. Thousands of serviceable aircraft were destroyed on their airfields and thousands of tanks burned in their own parks.

24

It may have been that Stalin spared Golikov in order to give him a testing assignment. He was certainly told to take himself abroad and revive and renew the GRU agent network which had been cut off immediately. He went first to England and then to the United States and, to give him his due, this time he succeeded in carrying out his work in an exemplary manner. For his visits to Great Britain and the United States he naturally did not use faked documents. He came, with a numerous entourage, as the head of an official Soviet military delegation to obtain American and British armaments. For the chief of the GRU and his colleagues the doors of secret factories and laboratories were opened – the very places Soviet intelligence had been trying for decades to penetrate. This historical visit was the beginning of intense penetration by Soviet military intelligence of the armaments industries of America and Britain. Golikov also succeeded, albeit only temporarily, in establishing communications with GRU illegals who were functioning on territory occupied by Germany; but this also signalled the beginning of GRU penetration of the German general staff from many different quarters. The consequences of this were that, beginning with Stalingrad, even top secret plans of the German High Command were known to Soviet front-line generals before they were known to the German field commanders. And the Soviet military leadership was equally enlightened as to the plans of its allies, the Americans and the British. Churchill bears witness to the fact that Stalin enumerated several points as to the contents of British top secret plans, though he attributes such enlightenment to Stalin's genius in foreseeing the future. The only thing that is not clear is why Stalin did not display a similar clairvoyancy with regard to Hitler's intentions in 1941 and the beginning of 1942.

In the autumn of 1941 Golikov returned from the United States, an another exceptionally successful visit. He could not, of course, expect to keep his post, but he stayed alive, and even kept his General's rank. On 13 October he was relieved of the command of the GRU and appointed commander of the 10th Army.

Later, in 1944, Stalin gave Golikov yet another chance to expiate his guilt with regard to the sudden German attack. In October he was appointed plenipotentiary of the Council of People's Commissars on Questions of the Repatriation of Soviet Citizens. At the same time as he was occupied with this task several of the former residents of the GRU in Europe were assigned to him. He acquitted himself again with great credit and, being able to count on the help of the GRU, succeeded in returning to the Soviet Union several million people who were practically all shot on arrival. Golikov's career was on the up and up, and he eventually reached the rank of Marshal of the Soviet Union.

In the autumn of 1941, after Golikov had relinquished his post, the GRU was divided into two. One of the newly-created organisations was directly answerable to Stalin and entitled the Chief Intelligence Directorate of the Supreme High Command. In the hands of this organisation was concentrated the agent network controlled by illegals and undercover residencies of the GRU in a small number of Soviet embassies. The 'other' GRU was subordinated to the general staff and preserved its former name of Chief Intelligence Directorate of the General Staff. But now this junior branch of the GRU co-ordinated the efforts of intelligence officers on all Soviet fronts in action against Germany. This new set-up was fully justified at that time. The GRU general staff was freed from having to make decisions on global problems which at that moment had lost their importance for the Soviet Union and instead was able to concentrate all its attention on carrying out intelligence operations against German forces. In order to distinguish between the two GRU's; the term 'strategic intelligence' was introduced for the first time and applied to the GRU of the Supreme Command, and the new title of 'operational intelligence' was given to the Intelligence Directorate of Fronts and the GRU of the general staff which controlled these directorates. Both the strategic and operational intelligence services of the Red Army conducted themselves with great distinction in the course of the war. The finest achievements of the strategic agent network were of course the penetration of the German general staff through Switzerland (via the illegal residency 'Dora') and the theft of American atomic secrets by way of Canada (through the residency 'Zaria'). Operational intelligence meanwhile developed activities unparalleled in scale. Besides its agent intelligence, a very large role was allocated to diversionary intelligence. Groups of guardminelayers were formed in the intelligence units of the fronts and armies whose basic purpose was to hunt down the German military staff. Parallel with these diversionary elements of the GRU, analogous groups of NKVD men were in action at the rear of the German forces. Between these two groups the traditional enmity fostered by the Party continued.

*

After the war, military intelligence was once again fused into one organisation, GRU General Staff, which independently carried out strategic intelligence and directed operational and tactical intelligence. At this time the Party and Stalin took care to weaken the Army and the Ministry of State Security, both of which had strengthened their positions during the war to such an extent that they had stopped acknowledging the civil leadership, i.e. the Party. The leading commanders, headed by Zhukov, were dismissed from the Army and Beria was also deprived of the leadership of the Tchekists. It would obviously not be a simple matter to expel him, so Stalin technically promoted him, appointing his deputy to succeed him, but in fact this deprived him of direct leadership of the Organs of State because his title of minister was taken away. Within the framework of the programme for weakening the Army and the Ministry of State Security, Stalin decided to remove intelligence from both the Army and State Security. This plan was put into effect in 1947. The GRU and the organs of political intelligence of the Ministry of State Security were joined together in one organisation called the KI: the Committee of Information. The man closest to Stalin was appointed to lead this organisation, and this was the activist of the Politburo, Molotov. Thus the Army and Ministry of State Security were deprived of intelligence. All intelligence work would henceforth be subordinate to the Party. Such a situation did not suit the Army or the Ministry of State Security, and they for the first time united against the Party.

From its inception the Committee of Information was an utterly ineffective organisation. The intelligence officers of the Ministry of State Security and the GRU, who formed the nucleus of the Committee of Information, strove by all means to return from under the control of the Party back to their own former organisations. Both sets of officers strove to sabotage the activities of the Committee of Information. The Ministry of State Security and the Army, acting in collusion, informed the Central Committee that they could no longer work effectively since they were receiving their information at second hand. Then they exerted pressure on

27

their former officers in order to try to make the Committee of Information collapse from inside. The Central Committee of the Party made efforts to improve the effectiveness of the Committee of Information. In less than a year four chiefs were appointed and dismissed, for the reason that not one of them was able to counter the unified strength of the Ministry of State Security and the Army. After long struggles behind the scenes Abakumov, a pupil and favourite of Beria, became Chief of the Committee of Information.

At a stroke, all the intelligence services passed to the control of the Ministry of State Security. Stalin immediately saw that a mistake had been made. In his opinion, the creation of one intelligence service, even if it was under the leadership of the Party, must sooner or later lead to the Tchekists seizing power over this organisation, and this would mortally endanger the Party. There was only one way out of such a situation: immediately to liquidate the Committee of Information and divide the intelligence service into two hostile camps – military intelligence to the Army, and political intelligence to State Security. But the coup was not an easy one. To get round the problem, the Party naturally found support from the Army which had not been at all happy with State Security's monopoly of the intelligence service. On the instructions of Stalin, the first deputy of the chief of the general staff, General Shtemyenko, made a report to the Politburo on the subject of the 'blind general staff', after which the GRU was removed from the control of Abakumov and given to the Army. For his distinguished services, Stalin immediately appointed General Shtemyenko as chief of the general staff—the senior curator of the GRU. After two years Shtemyenko and the GRU, seeking to please Stalin, presented documents about the existence of an agreement among subordinates of Abakumov. Abakumov was immediately shot, the Committee of Information finally abolished, and the usual purge carried out in the ranks of State Security.

But the Ministry of State Security did not forgive the general staff and the GRU for having taken such liberties. 1952 was a year of struggle between the Politburo and Stalin. The Ministry of State Security presented documents which they claimed proved the existence of a plot in the ranks of the GRU. This time it was the turn of the GRU and all the general staff to be purged. Stalin was opposed to the move, but the Politburo insisted. Shtemyenko was demoted to Lt-General and expelled from the general staff. The action continued against the general staff and the GRU, and even against Stalin himself who was removed as general secretary of the Communist Party later that year.

At the beginning of 1953, immediately after the death of Stalin, there ensued a fierce squabble among his disciples and comrades at arms for the distribution of the inheritance. The most dangerous pretender to the throne was, of course, Beria. The united strength of Army and Party was automatically against him. Beria was arrested at a joint session of Party and Army leaders and immediately done away with. After this there began the usual persecution of the Organs of State. During secret trials, incriminating documents were produced from the GRU concerning the leaders of the Ministry of State Security and many of its leaders were shot after frightful torture. The torture was carried out in the GRU cellars on Gogol Boulevard. At the beginning of 1954 the Ministry of State Security lost its status as a ministry and was transformed into a committee.

Simultaneously with the fall of the Ministry of State Security, the Army acquired more and more weight within the framework of the State. The 'Russian Bonaparte', Marshal Zhukov, became Minister of Defence, having returned from his exile under Stalin. After a short time Zhukov also became a member of the Politburo. He quickly effected the return of all the exiled generals and marshals and appointed them to key positions. The Ministry of State Security could not exercise any restraint on Zhukov and he was therefore able to appoint Shtemyenko to the post of Chief of the GRU, reinstating him as a full general after his demotion. The GRU became an organisation solely dependent on the Army. Zhukov's next step was a blow against Party influence in the Army. On his orders all political workers and Party commissars were expelled from the Army. He also ordered the Chief Political Directorate of the Soviet Army to stop interfering any more in Army affairs, and at the same time liquidated all the special departments of State Security present in the Army. The crocodile was clearly throwing off its bonds. In Politburo sessions Zhukov openly contradicted Khruschev and publicly abused him.

The Party understood how rashly it had behaved in depriving the KGB of power, since the Party alone was clearly defenceless against the Army. There was absolutely no doubt that very soon the Army would become the only master of the situation. But in October 1957 Zhukov committed a grave error. He went on a visit to Yugoslavia and in his absence, a plenum of the Central Committee of the Party was hurriedly convened. Zhukov was secretly removed from the Politburo and also from his duties as Minister of Defence because of 'bonapartism'. The chief of the GRU, General Shtemyenko, learned about what had happened and immediately sent a telegram of warning to Zhukov in Yugoslavia, but it was intercepted by the KGB. Zhukov returned from Yugoslavia straight into renewed exile. Shtemyenko followed him, again reduced to the rank of lieutenant-general. (Some survive vicissitudes better than others: under Brezhnev, Shtemyenko was again reinstated.)

*

Now once more the post of chief of the GRU was held by a member of the KGB, Ivan Serov. Henceforth everything would go according to Lenin's teachings. Serov, on his appointment, automatically turned into an arch-rival and enemy of the KGB, and was not in the least interested in the fusion of these two organisations. But since he had been a general of the KGB, the Army could not exploit him against the Party and the KGB. That was not all. In order to control the Army in the interests of the Party, General Golikov, the former chief of the GRU, was appointed chief of the Political Directorate of the Soviet Army. Golikov was a former Tchekist and political worker and he was ready to serve anybody who desired his services and to report only the data which would please the leadership. Such a person was eminently suitable as far as the Party was concerned.

Serov's successor as chief of the GRU was Colonel-General of the KGB, Petr Ivashutin. General Yepishev, who had been from 1951 to 1953 Deputy Minister of State Security, succeeded Golikov as chief of the Political Directorate of the Soviet Army. In a word, the crocodile was again firmly on the leash.

Chapter Three

The Pyramid

If we approach the term GRU in a formal way in order to explain everything that is covered by those three letters, we shall get a very impressive picture but one that is far from complete. To look at the GRU in isolation from its subordinate organisations is to look at Gengis Khan without his innumerable hordes.

The GRU may formally be described as an immensely powerful intelligence organisation forming part of the general staff and acting in the interests of the higher military command of the Soviet Union. On its strength there are more than five thousand senior officers and generals who have specialist academic qualifications in intelligence matters. The GRU has its illegal representatives in every country of the world. In addition, officers of the GRU operate under cover in every country of the world as diplomats, military attachés, trade representatives and so on. Both the illegals and the undercover officers independently from each other carry out the recruitment of agents, who then, under the direction of the GRU steal top-secret documents, axe governments and kill statesmen. The central apparatus of the GRU processes espionage information coming from a thousand secret agents and it also carries out cosmic, electronic, air and sea intelligence on a global scale.

But we have not mentioned the most important point yet. Up to now we are talking about Gengis Khan but not his hordes. What is more important is that, in addition to all this, in addition to carrying out intelligence work in the interests of the general staff, the GRU is also the superior directing organ of the gigantic formation called Soviet military intelligence.

Organisationally, the Soviet Army consists of sixteen military districts, four 'groups of forces' – in Germany, Poland, Hungary and Czechoslovakia – and four fleets – the Northern, Pacific, Black

Sea and Baltic fleets. On the staff strengths of each district, group and fleet there are intelligence directorates. In all, these directorates number twenty-four. They are all subject to the GRU and are, in effect, a GRU in miniature. Each of these mini-GRU's utilises its own facilities. With all the forces at their disposal, they gather information on the enemy, both in peace-time and wartime.

When we speak of an intelligence directorate of a district, group or fleet as a mini-GRU, this does not in the least mean that the intelligence directorate is small or weak. We only mean that the intelligence directorates (RU) of staffs are smaller than the chief directorate of the general staff. But each of these twenty-four intelligence directorates is sufficiently strong to be able to recruit agents independently in the territories of countries or groups of countries which are in the sphere of interest of the given district, group or fleet. Each intelligence directorate possesses sufficient power to be able, without assistance, to disrupt life in any contiguous country or group of countries. There is only one form of intelligence possessed by the GRU which the intelligence directorates do not possess, and this is cosmic or space intelligence. At the same time, instead of this, they have a perhaps no less important means, which are the diversionary *Spetsnaz* units. In addition to ordinary agents providing secret information, the intelligence directorates recruit special agent-terrorists destined to murder statesmen or senior military officers and to carry out general terror in the country or group of countries. Thus each district, group of forces or fleet has its own two independent secret agent networks, the first being the ordinary espionage network, and the second the espionage-terrorist network called *Spetsnaz*. To visualize the strength of one intelligence directorate, it is sufficient to remember that each one controls an entire *Spetsnaz* brigade: 1,300 professional cut-throats continually in readiness to penetrate the territory of a contiguous state and go to the assistance of the agent-terrorists.

One can best imagine Soviet military intelligence in the form of a powerful, feudal state – the GRU – with a first-class army. There are twenty-four lesser satellite states, the intelligence directorates (RU), subordinated to the head of this state, and each of these in its turn has its own army, and a strong one at that. But each satellite also has its vassals each of whom has his own army and his own vassals, also with armies, and so forth. The only difference as regards this pyramid form of subordination is that Soviet military intelligence does not operate on the principle that 'the vassal of my vassal is not my vassal'. The GRU fully and without delegating authority controls every step of the pyramid. These steps need to be examined.

Each military district and group of forces consists of armies. Each fleet consists of flotillas which are equivalent to the armies of the land forces. On the staff of each army there is an intelligence department (RO) which is in effect a full vassal of the superior intelligence directorate and the still superior chief intelligence directorate. The intelligence department (RO) of an army or flotilla does run an agent network of its own. On the strength of each intelligence department, and there are in the Soviet armed forces at least fifty, there is a *Spetsnaz* company. This company, which numbers 115 saboteurs and cut-throats, is capable of penetrating into the enemy's territory to murder and kidnap people, blow up bridges, electric power stations, dams, oil pipelines and so on. And these *Spetsnaz* units are supplemented by the intelligence department's wide choice of electronic, air and other types of intelligence.

An army in the Soviet Union consists of from four to six divisions. In peace-time there are in the Soviet armed forces about 180 tank and motorised divisions. In the interests of simplification we can omit the eight divisions of airborne forces (VDV), the brigades of marine infantry belonging to the fleets and still many more branches of the Soviet Army which have intelligence units subordinated directly to the GRU of the general staff. On the strength of the staff of each division there is a chief reconnaissance officer. He has his own troops, a reconnaissance battalion, and his vassals, the heads of regimental reconnaissance and their troops. The reconnaissance battalion of each division, apart from tank and electronic reconnaissance, has a sabotage company which is also staffed with cut-throats capable of successful operations in the enemy's rear. In the interests of accuracy it is necessary to add that not all of the 180 tank and motorised rifle divisions have a full complement of personnel in peace-time; many of them have a complete technical staff and full officer strength, but only a partial complement of soldiers and NCOs. However, this rule does not apply to reconnaissance units. All the

Spetsnaz brigades and companies of the military districts and armies, all the reconnaissance battalions (180) of the divisions, all the regimental reconnaissance companies (more than 700), are always kept at full strength and staffed by élite officers and NCOs.

Everything that we have listed comes under the indivisible control of the GRU, although none of it is called by this name. The researcher who studies the GRU but does not take into consideration the GRU's vassals will have overlooked twenty-four separate espionage organisations, each of which is as powerful as the intelligence service of one central European country. He will have overlooked 100,000 élite troops possessing as many fighting vehicles as a well-equipped Western European country. But even that is not all. In addition to its official vassals the GRU also has unofficial vassals who carry out the orders of the GRU as precisely and with as much jealous zeal as do the intelligence directorates of military districts, the intelligence departments of armies and the chief reconnaissance officers of divisions and regiments. These are the military intelligence services of Cuba, Poland, East Germany, Czechoslovakia, Hungary, Bulgaria, Mongolia and a number of other countries. These countries are satellites and in the full meaning of the word vassals of the Soviet Union. Their secret police forces are under the complete control of the Soviet KGB and take the form of a miniature copy of the KGB. Their armies are in thrall to the Soviet Army and their military intelligence services are full vassals of the GRU, with all their agents, illegals, military attachés, sabotage agents, diversionary troops and so on. But of these later.

Chapter Four

The GRU and the Military Industrial Commission (VPK)

When we use the term 'army' with regard to the Soviet Army we must have in mind not only the Ministry of Defence, but also the twelve other ministries whose sole function it is to produce weapons and military technology. Together all these ministries form the high-powered monolith headed by the military industrial commission (VPK). Included in the collegium of the military industrial commission are: one of the first deputies of the chairman of the council of ministers, thirteen ministers, and the chief of the general staff and the chief of the GRU. The military industrial commission is the Army and the Army is the military industrial commission. When we talk of a struggle between the Army and the Party and the KGB we have in mind the struggle of the whole military industrial commission, whose fortunes wax and wane in perfect harmony with the Army's own.

The economic and financial might of the military industrial commission can only be compared with the might of the Soviet Union itself. Theoretically the Soviet Union spends, in the interests of defence, the improbably small sum of nineteen billion roubles a year. This nineteen billion, however, is the budget of the Ministry of Defence alone. The budgets of the remaining twelve ministries which produce armaments are kept secret. The Soviet system is constructed in such a way that the Ministry of Defence does not buy; it receives the armaments necessary to it. For example, an aircraft carrier is under construction in the Soviet Union. The Ministry of Defence does not bear any of the cost of this. The price of the ship is paid to the Ministry of Shipbuilding by the Council of Ministers under the debit item 'shipbuilding industry'. This Ministry, by the way, has never constructed any non-military vessels. Non-military vessels are, without exception, bought for the Soviet Union in Poland, East Germany, Yugoslavia, Bulgaria, Italy, France, Norway, Sweden, Denmark – it is difficult indeed to list all of them. It is probably true that only Switzerland is an exception to this list. The same thing is true of aircraft, tanks, rockets, nuclear bombs. military electronics, every item of hardware. Nobody in the Soviet Union knows exactly how much the military industrial commission swallows up, but in any case it is an astronomical figure.

At the heart of any Soviet five-year plan for economic development – not the propaganda plan which appears in all the newspapers, but the genuine, secret plan – will be found the military industrial commission's plan. For all the other branches of the Soviet economy, metallurgy, machine tool construction, energy, transport, agriculture, have no independent significance but only provide for the activities of the military industrial commission. Soviet science is another organ providing for the military industrial commission. Officially it is allocated about sixty billion roubles a year, three times more than defence. But what sort of science is it, if the Soviet Union can produce the first automatic satellite destroyer in the world but cannot produce an ordinary compact, small-engined car? The Soviet Union has had to buy all its technology for the production of small cars from Italy. What are Soviet scientists up to if the Soviet Union has first-class military poisons but has to buy fertiliser technology from the United States? What are the sixty billion roubles spent on if the USSR constructs gigantic trans-horizontal radar, ultra-high frequency transmitters for communications with submarines whose underground aerials amount to thousands of kilometres in length – but has to buy the technology for the production of ordinary household television sets from France? Sixty billion roubles on science is yet another means of camouflaging Soviet military expenditure and the true might of the military industrial commission.

What has the GRU to do with this? The connection is this: the budget of the GRU is many times greater than the budget of the KGB. But the KGB is much bigger than the GRU, it has a vast apparatus within the country and its political influence is colossal. So why is the financial might of the GRU many times greater than that of the KGB? (Some specialists consider it to be several tens of times greater.) The business may be explained as follows. The KGB has its budget, which is without doubt enormous, and the GRU also has a moderate budget. Both form a part of State expenses and naturally the State tries to limit these expenses. But in addition to its 'clean' budget the GRU has colossal orders from the military industrial commission and from Soviet science which provides for the military commission. These orders are incalculably greater than the actual 'clean' budget of the GRU. For example, on receiving an order from the military industrial commission to steal a tank engine, the GRU receives money allocated as a debit item to 'science' or 'industry'. With this money the GRU will recruit an agent without spending a single cent of its own money, industry and science will receive the engine they want and save enormous expense, and finally the GRU's 'free' agent will continue to work on its behalf for the rest of his life. All twelve ministries of the military industrial commission, plus all of military science, are ready to place money with the GRU if only they can obtain the technology which is essential to them. Designers and factory directors receive medals and prizes for copying foreign samples of armaments in the same way as they would if they worked out their own examples. The KGB depends only on its actual budget, but the GRU draws on the budget of all Soviet armament industries and science. In the course of a major GRU operation, such as the theft of all the technological documentation for the American nuclear submarine *George Washington* (which enabled the Soviet Union to build a perfect copy — nicknamed 'Small George'), the GRU will not spend a single dollar of its own budget. Other memorable examples were the copying of the American missile 'Red Eye' and the Anglo-French Concorde, among many others

*

Why does the KGB not carry out orders for the armaments industry? This is very simple. The chairmen of the Council of Ministers and Gosplan* are responsible for the Soviet economy. They plan how much money to allocate, to whom and for what purpose. To the chairman of the Council of Ministers are subordinated both the armaments industry and the Minister of Defence with the general staff and the GRU. The KGB, alas, is not answerable to the chairman of the Council of Ministers. Having given money to the

* The State planning committee.

GRU to obtain something interesting, the chairman of the Council of Ministers or the chairman of the military industrial commission may bang on the table and demand that delivery be speeded up. But if they give money to the KGB then they will have to wait quietly until the KGB is ready to deliver the goods. The KGB is not usually in much of a hurry, even when it has been handsomely and generously paid. The KGB is a vain and arrogant courtier, having the right to speak at the King's council, but without a sou in his pocket. The GRU is an ugly hunchback: a moneylender, ready to serve anybody and making millions in the process. The courtier hates the moneylender. The courtier would kill the moneylender were it not for the fact that he serves the King himself.

Chapter Five

But Why is Nothing Known about it?

In the Soviet Union the registration plates of certain cars from Georgia end with the letters GRU. This amusing coincidence goes unnoticed by almost everybody, including the police, for the GRU is unknown in the Soviet Union except to a small circle of enlightened ones. Even in the general staff, of which the GRU is a part, thousands of colonels simply consider that 'military department 44388', whence comes all espionage information, is a branch of the KGB. Moreover, KGB officers who guard Soviet embassies overseas but are not members of the KGB intelligence organisation consider, in many cases, that there is only one residency in the embassy, that of the KGB.

Much is known about the GRU by Western specialists, but the ordinary Western man in the street has practically no idea at all about it. His attitude is analogous to his attitude to the mythical animal from a Scottish loch: either it exists, there have been photographs published of it, or then again perhaps it does not exist. Some believe, others do not, but decidedly nobody is frightened of the animal. Nevertheless, how can so little be known about the GRU, given that it certainly exists and certainly possesses colossal power?

There are quite a few reasons, so let us discuss the most important ones. Firstly, having established their bloody dictatorship, the communists had to announce to the people the existence of an 'extraordinary' organ of the dictatorship of the proletariat which was permitted to deal in whatever way it pleased with the people – including the mass executions of millions. They did this through the mouth of Lenin when he informed the people about the birth of the V. Tcheka. Later Lenin's successors informed people of all the changes in the names of the Organs, underlining that it was only the nomenclature that changed. The essence remained as before. Traditions live, and it is still forbidden to complain about the Organs. The GRU did not need such publicity and therefore nothing official was given out about its existence. Secondly, the main function of the Organs is to exert pressure on the people themselves. Consequently in the people's consciousness everything that is dark, underground and secret is connected with the KGB but not at all with the GRU. In practical terms the GRU did not take part in the struggle against the people. Not because it was full of humanity and love for its fatherland, but simply because nobody had given it this function. Naturally people remember the KGB (on any pretext), but never the GRU. Thirdly, in his struggle for power, Kruschev made known to a stunned world some of the crimes of his predecessors and honourable Tchekists. The effect was so shattering that from that moment the whole world unreservedly saw the leadership of the KGB in all spheres of secret criminal activity. Kruschev by no means revealed everything, but only that which at a given moment might bring him undoubted political capital. He pointed to the mass executions in Stalin's time but forgot to mention the mass executions in Lenin's time. He mentioned the destruction of the communist leaders in 1937 but omitted the destruction of the peasants in 1930. He demonstrated the role of the NKVD but completely forgot the role of the communist party as the main, leading and directing force. Kruschev was interested in showing up the crimes of the Organs within the country and he did show up several of them. Revelations of crimes committed overseas did not enter into Kruschev's plans. They could not bring him any political advantage. He was therefore silent in this regard and did not mention the overseas crimes of the KGB and, of course, those of the GRU. Fourthly, the struggles against dissent, emigration, and western radio stations broadcasting to the Soviet Union are the sole responsibility of the KGB but not the GRU. Naturally the most talented representatives of liberation movements and immigration address their best efforts to enlightening the KGB itself. It is the same as regards radio station broadcasting to the Soviet Union and the Western organs of mass information in general. They certainly devote to the KGB significantly greater attention. Fifthly, any unpleasant things which happen to foreigners in the Soviet Union are first and foremost connected with the KGB and this gives rise to a corresponding flow of information about the

KGB. Lastly, having made rivers of blood from the people, the KGB strove to whitewash itself at all costs advertising the 'attainments' of the Tchekists. In this connection all intelligence officers, KGB or GRU, were categorised as Tchekists, and this at a time when GRU intelligence officers hated the Tchekists many times more than they did the Gestapo. The GRU did not object to this. It preferred to maintain silence, not only about its crimes and mistakes, but also about its successes. The spying breed of animal keeps itself in the depths; muddy water and darkness are more to its liking than publicity.

Chapter Six

The GRU and the 'Younger Brothers'

The state structure of any communist country strikingly resembles the structure of the Soviet Union. Even if it finds itself in conflict with the Soviet Union or has been able to escape from its influence, it is much the same in character. The cult of personality is a general rule for all communist countries, and any 'big brother' needs an all-powerful secret police force to preserve that cult. Then there must be another secret organisation to counter-balance the power of the first one.

It is usually military intelligence which fulfils this counter-balancing role, the more so since all communist countries, regardless of the kind of communism they adopt, are warlike and aggressive. In a number of communist countries there would appear to be only one secret police organisation, but in these cases closer inspection will clearly show a minimum of two mutually hostile groupings. Sooner or later the dictator will be forced to split his secret service into two parts. In the countries within the orbit of the Soviet Union that separation has already been carried out, for all of them have been created in the image of the elder brother.

The military intelligence services of the satellite countries show great activity in the collection of espionage material, and all such material obtained is sent directly to the GRU. The fact is that the intelligence services of the satellite countries are even legally answerable to the Ministry of Defence of the Soviet Union. The military intelligence service of each Warsaw Pact country is subordinate to its chief of the general staff, but the chief of staff is in his turn subordinate to the chief of staff of the Warsaw Pact. Theoretically a general from any country of the Warsaw Pact may be appointed to this position. In practice of course there have only ever been Soviet generals appointed. One of them is already well known to us: the former chief of the GRU, General Shtemyenko. After the fall of Kruschev, Brezhnev, trying to please the Army, recalled the disgraced general from exile and reinstated him as a full general. As chief of staff of the Warsaw Pact, his direct superior was (and is) the High Commander of the United Armed Forces of the member-countries. To this post it has always been a Soviet marshal who has been appointed. First it was Konyev, then Grechko, after him Yakubovski and finally Kulikov. But the official title of all these marshals during the time they commanded the united forces was 'First Deputy of the Minister of Defence of the USSR – Commander-in-Chief of the United Armed Forces of the member countries of the Warsaw Pact'. In other words, the armies are the armies of several states subordinated to a deputy minister of defence in one of those states. There is sovereignty for you. The USSR Minister of Defence, through his deputy, directs all the forces of staffs of the 'fraternal countries', including, of course, the military intelligence services of those countries, and we are not talking of close co-operation, but of direct subordination in the legal sense.

This is all very well, some sceptics will object, but after what happened in 1939, every Pole had a fierce dislike for the Soviet communists, and their intelligence services would hardly work their best in the interests of the GRU, would they? After 1953 the East Germans fully shared the feelings of the Poles. In 1956 Hungary joined them, and in 1968 the Czechs and Slovaks. Surely the intelligence services of these countries would not work hard in the interests of Soviet military intelligence? Unfortunately this is a delusion which has gained too wide an acceptance. In practice everything contradicts it. It *is* a fact that the peoples of all countries in thrall to the Soviet Union hate the Soviet communists; but none the less their intelligence services work to the full extent of their powers in the interests of the elder brother. The solution to the riddle is this. By means of harsh economic treaties the Soviet Union has enchained all its 'younger brothers'. For Soviet oil and coal, electric energy and gas they all have to pay very heavily. The Soviet Union proposes to its satellites that 'you may pay by means of your own wares or you may pay by providing the secrets of other people'. This alternative offer is a very tempting one, to which the general secretaries have unanimously responded by ordering their intelligence officers to redouble their efforts. So the intelligence services of all countries tied economically to the Soviet Union make the greatest possible efforts. By stealing Western secrets and transmitting them to Soviet military or political intelligence they reduce their countries' indebtedness and raise their peoples' standards of living.

Western states have been surprised by the extent of the intelligence interests of communist states. Why should Mongolian intelligence be interested in atomic reactors, or Cuban intelligence in high-powered rocket engines? These questions are easily answered as soon as one realises that they are all part of one gigantic formation. In the ranks of officials of Soviet state institutions overseas it is almost impossible to find one 'clean' one. All Soviet citizens, from ambassadors to cleaning staff, in one way or another co-operate with the KGB or the GRU. The same thing is true of the official institutions of the 'fraternal countries'. There it is also difficult to find a single 'clean' official. All of them are to some extent co-operating with the Soviet KGB or GRU – even though frequently they themselves do not realise it.

Chapter Seven

The GRU and the KGB

The working methods of the GRU and the KGB are absolutely identical. It is impossible to tell their signatures apart. But their functions differ essentially one from the other. The basic function of the KGB may be expressed in one guiding phrase, *not to allow the collapse of the Soviet Union from inside*. Every specific function stems from this. To enumerate some of those functions: the protection of communist VIPs; the suppression of any clashes or dissent among the population; the carrying out of censorship and disinformation; the prohibition of any contact between the people and the outside world – including the isolation of foreign visitors – and the cutting off of any contacts already established with them; and the guarding of frontiers (there are ten districts of KGB frontier forces). The KGB also acts overseas but its activities rotate around the same main axis – to prevent the collapse of the USSR from within. This task can be divided in the same way into its parts: the struggle with emigration and efforts to diminish its influence on the internal life of the Soviet Union; the struggle with Western radio stations broadcasting to the Soviet Union and other means of mass information which give a correct picture of the situation 'within the state of workers and peasants'; the struggle with religious organisations which might exert influence on the Soviet population; observing the 'fraternal' communist parties with the aim of nipping in the bud any heresy which might emerge from them; the surveillance of all Soviet citizens abroad, including KGB officers themselves; the seeking out and destruction of the most active opponents of the communist regime. The KGB also has other functions, but these are all either a part of the main function or not of prime importance.

The function of the GRU may also be stated in one parallel, but quite different phrase: *to prevent the collapse of the Soviet Union from an external blow*. In the opinion of the general staff such a blow may be struck at the Soviet Union in peace-time, even in the course of routine Soviet military adventures in Asia, Africa or Europe. This, the most important function of the GRU, is undertaken on four fronts. On the *military* front, literally everything is of interest to the GRU. Of prime importance, of course, are the composition, quantity and deployment of the armed forces of all countries of the world; the plans and thinking of the military leadership and staffs; mobilisation plans in case of war; the type and direction of military training of forces; the organisation of forces; the means of supply; morale and so on. Of prime importance on the *military-political* front are the relations between the different countries of the world: overt and covert disagreements; possible changes in political and military leadership of military and economic blocs; new alliances; any, even the slightest, change in the political and military orientation of armies, governments, countries and whole blocs and alliances. On the *military-technological* front the GRU handles intelligence related to the development of new kinds of armaments and military technique in the countries of a probable enemy; the carrying out of trials and tests; new technological processes which might be utilised for military ends. And the *military-economic* front presents exceptional interest for the GRU. First and foremost it is fascinated by the capacity of such and such a state or group of states to produce modern types of weapons, but it is also extremely keen to learn about industrial potential, energy, transport, agriculture, the presence of strategic reserves, vulnerable areas of economy, and energy. The general staff considers that if the GRU can give accurate information in good time from every country in the world on these four fronts, then it can count it impossible to destroy the Soviet Union by means of a blow from outside.

In many instances the interests of the KGB and the GRU are diametrically different. For example, a demonstration of White Russian émigrés is of absolutely no interest to the GRU, but an object of the greatest possible interest to the KGB. And vice-versa: no military exercises are of any interest to the KGB residents, but they are of great interest to GRU residents. Even in those fields where the GRU and the KGB have what would seem to be interests in common, for example in politics, their approach to a particular problem would differ in essence. For example, the personality of

President Carter from the very beginning provoked almost no interest from the side of the GRU, for on the most superficial possible examination of the President's personality the GRU infallibly decided that he would never be the first to carry out a pre-emptive strike against the Soviet Union. But that same man, from the point of view of the KGB, appears to be the most dangerous opponent possible, because his human rights policies are a weapon which could destroy the Soviet Union from within. In another case, the GRU displayed exceptional interest in the changes of personnel in the Chinese political and military leadership. For the KGB this question posed practically no interest at all. The KGB very well knows that after sixty years of communist power the Soviet population will not be in the least interested in any communist ideology from China or Korea or Yugoslavia; it is also quite convinced that not one defector from the Soviet Union will ever seek refuge in China. China is, for the KGB, almost an empty place.

In examining mutual relations between the GRU and the KGB we have to return to the question of the GRU's dependence on the KGB. In the chapter on history we endeavoured to show the character of these mutual relations in the past. The same mutual relations have been preserved up to the present day. The GRU and the KGB are ready at any moment to destroy each other. Between them exist exactly those mutual relations which perfectly suit the Party. The jealousy and mutual hatred between the GRU and KGB are familiar to the police of every country where the Soviet Union has an embassy, and it is precisely this enmity, noticeable even to 'unarmed eyes', which provides proof of the independence of the GRU.

If the fate or career of a GRU resident were to depend even slightly on his colleague from the KGB, he would never in his life dare to differ with, still less quarrel or brawl with, the Tchekists: he would be like a cowed lap-dog with his tail between his legs, not even daring to bark for the lady of the house, like the 'clean' diplomats in all Soviet embassies. But officers of the GRU do not do this. They have guarantees of their independence and invulnerability from the KGB. Some specialists are inclined to consider the GRU as a branch of the KGB, usually adducing in defence of this opinion two arguments. Firstly, they say that the chief of the GRU is always a former KGB general, but this has always been the case, beginning with Aralov, and has never prevented the GRU from actively opposing the efforts of the KGB to swallow it, and even sometimes on the order of the Party striking the Tchekists sudden and heavy blows. The second argument is that everybody joining the GRU has to be vetted by the KGB. This argument appears convincing only at a first glance. The fact is that each new official of the Central Committee of the Party also undergoes the same vetting by the KGB, but it certainly does not follow this that the Central Committee is under the control of the KGB or is a branch of the KGB. Both the Central Committee and the GRU select for themselves the people necessary to them, and in this connection consult the KGB, for any person until he becomes a Central Committee official or joins the GRU is under the control of the KGB and possibly the KGB may have some unfavourable information on a given person. The KGB in this case plays the part of a filter. But once having passed this person through its filter the KGB no longer has the right to interfere with him, either inside the Central Committee or inside the GRU. The KGB is like a guard at the gate of a secret installation. The guard may refuse entry to an engineer who has forgotten his pass at home, but he has no right to examine the contents of that engineer's safe. If it so desires, the KGB may, of course, discredit any unwanted official of the GRU or the Central Committee. However, this is fraught with potential reciprocal measures.

There exists still another irrefutable indicator of the independence of the GRU from the KGB. In the GRU there is no 'special department'. The security of the GRU is assured by its own forces, and always has been. The Party is very keen that this should continue, because it knows that if the KGB were to organise its own 'special department' in the GRU, a similar department would swiftly be introduced into the Politburo.

To illustrate the uneasy peace and the paradox of the independence that exists within the triangle of Party – KGB – GRU, let us consider a real confrontation. The working day of the GRU chief usually begins at seven o'clock in the morning, sometimes earlier. At that time he personally reads all telegrams which have come during the night from illegals, from undercover residencies, and from the intelligence directorates of military districts, groups of forces and of the fleet intelligence. In the next-door office, the first deputy to the GRU chief and the chief of information of the GRU are doing the same thing. If any questions have been raised by any of the higher commanders, from the chief of the general staff upwards, their opinions will be heard separately, independent from the opinions of the GRU chief.

This day began for the GRU leadership at the unusually early hour of 3.30 in the morning, when it was informed by the command point that the aircraft from Paris had landed at the central airport and taxied up to the GRU building. The day before, at Le Bourget airport, the Soviet supersonic passenger aircraft Tupolev TU144 had crashed. The whole of the Paris residency had been at the show and the majority had had ciné cameras. The moment of catastrophe had been photographed from different points by different officers, and the GRU had at its disposal no fewer then twenty films showing the same moment. The films had not been developed in Paris but brought straight to Moscow. Now the operational technological institute of the GRU would develop them immediately. At nine o'clock in the morning the Politburo session was to begin, at which they would hear evidence from Tupolev, his deputies, the minister of aviation production, the director of the Voronesh aviation factory, directors of subsidiary concerns, test pilots and of course the GRU and the KGB. But at seven, the telephone rang and it was Andropov, at the time head of the KGB. 'Peter Ivanovitch, how are you?'

Peter Ivanovitch Ivashutin (present chief of the GRU) did not hasten to match the friendly tone. 'Well. How are you, comrade Andropov?'

'Peter Ivanovitch, don't be so official. Have you forgotten my name? Peter Ivanovitch, there is something I want to talk to you about. I hear you have got some films showing the catastrophe.' Peter Ivanovitch said nothing. 'Peter Ivanovitch, would you be very kind and give me just one little film? You know yourself that I have to make a report to the Politburo but I have no material. These shows are not of great interest to my chaps and unfortunately not one of them was there with a ciné camera. Help me to get out of this mess. I need that film about the catastrophe.'

All service telephone calls to the GRU chief are relayed through the GRU command point. The duty shift of operators is always in readiness to prompt their chief with a necessary figure or fact, or to help him over a mistake in conversation. At this point the entire duty shift was frozen to the spot. Their help was not called for at all. The GRU chief remained silent for some time. The duty operators were quite certain that in a similar situation, the KGB would undoubtedly refuse if the GRU asked for its help. But what would be the decision of the GRU chief, an ex-colonel-general of the KGB and ex-deputy chairman of the KGB? Finally, in friendly, even tones he answered Andropov.

'Yuri Vladimirovich, I won't give you one film, I'll give you all twenty. Only I will show them at nine o'clock in the Politburo, and at ten o'clock I'll send my chaps over to the Central Committee to give you all the films.'

Andropov angrily slammed down the receiver. A concerted roar of laughter shook the walls of the underground command point. The senior operator, choking with laughter, entered the conversation in the log book.

(After Andropov became General Secretary of the Communist Party and Soviet Leader, Ivashutin still survived as GRU chief, because any attack from Andropov could easily have upset the fragile Party-Army balance with unpredictable consequences for Andropov himself.)

Chapter Eight

The Centre

Unlike the KGB, the GRU does not try to advertise itself, and its head office does not rise in the centre of the capital on its most crowded square. The head office of the GRU, although it is in Moscow, is by no means easy to find. It is enclosed from three sides by the central airport, the old Khodinka field. The aerodrome is surrounded on all sides by restricted buildings, among which are the offices of three leading aviation firms and one rocket construction firm, and the military aviation academy and the aviation institute. In the centre of these secret institutes the aerodrome carries on with its life as if half-asleep. Very, very rarely, in the middle of the night, a covered-up fuselage of a fighter aircraft is taken out of a hangar, loaded onto a transport aeroplane and transported somewhere into the trans-Volga steppe for testing. Sometimes another transport aircraft lands, goes up to the GRU building and unloads a foreign tank or rocket, after which everything becomes peaceful again. For two months of the year preparations are carried out for the grandiose military parades, and the roar of tank engines can be heard on the airfield. The parades finish, but the guarded area remains guarded, an empty field in the centre of Moscow patrolled by watchdogs. Not one civil aircraft or helicopter disturbs the quiet of Khodinka, only the watchdogs howl at night like wolves. How many of them are there? One loses count. No, from three sides it is impossible to get to the GRU. From the fourth side, too. On the fourth side there is the Institute of Cosmic Biology, with more dogs and electric barbed wire. A narrow little lane leads through a blind wall ten metres high, behind which is the 'Aquarium'. In order to penetrate into the inner fortress of the GRU one must negotiate either the area of the secret aerodrome or the area of the top secret institute.

The head office of the GRU is a nine-storey extended rectangle.

On all sides the building is surrounded by a two-storey structure, the windows of which give onto the central courtyard. The external walls have no windows at all. The fifteen-storey building adjacent to the area also belongs to the GRU, although it is situated outside its external walls. Many families of GRU officers live here, and the building has a completely normal appearance and looks like an ordinary block of flats. Only a certain number of the flats, however, are used for living purposes; the others are used by the service for official purposes. The whole of the area, centimetre by centimetre, is under surveillance from the tele-cameras and patrolled continuously by gentlemen with big, fat faces. But even if it were not thus, a stranger there would be apprehended immediately. Any of the little old men seated on benches (minimum twenty years' service in the GRU) would immediately inform the necessary people if he saw something untoward. Nobody is allowed to bring a car into the GRU's inner area, not even the Minister of Defence or General Secretary. One is only admitted after passing through a special inspection and sophisticated electronic equipment. Nobody may bring in so much as a cigarette lighter, still less a briefcase. There must be no metallic object on your person, not even a belt-buckle – the GRU recommends braces. All necessities for work and life are to be found inside, including cigarette lighters and fountain pens. The GRU gives them out – after they have been checked, of course.

*

The chief of the GRU is subordinate to the chief of the general staff and is his deputy. Directly subordinate to the chief of the GRU are the GRU's command point, the deputy chief and a group of advisers. The organisational units constituting the GRU are directorates, directions, and sections. In units which are not directly concerned with the acquisition and processing of information there exist the divisions of directorates, departments and sections. The military rank of the chief of the GRU is Army General. Under him are a first deputy and deputies. In the case where the deputy has several directorates under his command, his military rank will be colonel-general. If he only has one directorate, lieutenant-general. Chiefs of directorates are lieutenant-generals. The deputies of heads of directorates, heads of directions and departments are major-generals. The deputy

1. GRU: Internal structure

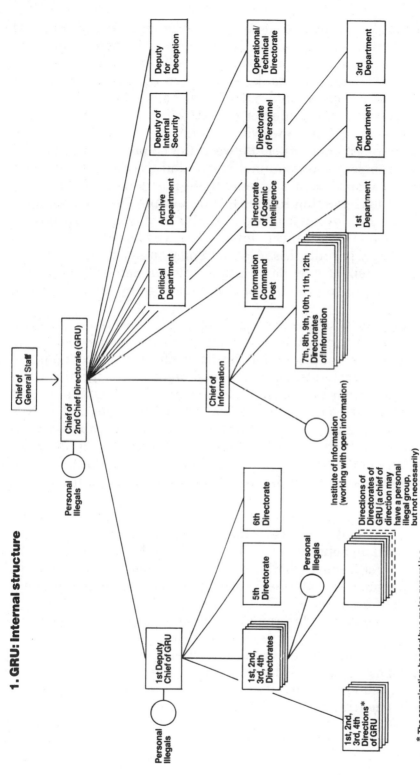

heads of directions and departments, the heads of sections and their deputies are colonels. The rank-and-file members of sections are called senior operational officers and operational officers. The military rank of a senior operational officer is colonel, of an operational officer lieutenant-colonel.

An overwhelming number of GRU officers hold the military rank of colonel. This, however, does not at all mean that they are equal amongst each other. Between the colonel who fulfils the duties of a senior operational officer and the deputy head of a direction who is also a colonel there is a wide gulf. The high service ranks existing in the GRU do not preclude the appointment of a very young captain or senior lieutenant to the post of senior operational officer, either. The system adopted by the Soviet Army permits this. A captain may be an acting major, or a senior lieutenant may be an acting colonel. Seniority is judged not by the pips on the officer's shoulder, but by the position he holds.

In total the GRU has sixteen directorates: most of them have a number from one to twelve. Certain numbers do not exist and the directorate is simply called by its name, as for example the personnel directorate. Directions and departments forming parts of a directorate have numbers, for example '41 Direction' means the first direction of the fourth directorate. Directions and departments not forming part of a directorate have a single number with the letters GRU added, for example, the first department GRU. The hierarchy in the GRU is as follows. The chief of the GRU has one first deputy and seven deputies beneath him. He controls:

i   The Illegals Section. With the help of this section he personally directs effective illegals and agents about whom nobody knows. He also directs his own first deputy.

ii   First Deputy Chief of the GRU (colonel-general), beneath whom are all the procurement organs which provide information.

iii The Chief of Information (colonel-general) in charge of all the processing organs of the GRU.

iv   The Chief of the Political Section (lieutenant-general).

v   The Chief of the Electronic Intelligence Directorate (lieutenant-general).

vi   The Chief of Fleet Intelligence (vice-admiral).

vii   The Chief of the Cosmic Intelligence Directorate (lieutenant-general).

viii   The Head of the Soviet Army Academy (colonel-general).

ix   The Head of the Personnel Directorate (lieutenant-general).

Chapter Nine

The Procurement Organs

All units of the GRU are divided in their designations into procurement, processing and support. The great majority of the procurement organs, the providers of information, are controlled by the first deputy chief of the GRU. They include the first directorate, which carries out agent intelligence on European territory, and consists of five directions, each of which carries out agent intelligence on the territories of several countries (each direction consists of sections which direct undercover residencies in one of the countries concerned); the second directorate with an analogous organisation carrying out agent intelligence in America, both North and South; the third directorate, which carries out agent intelligence in Asia; and the fourth directorate, dealing with agent intelligence in Africa, and the Middle East. Each directorate contains about 300 high-ranking officers in the Moscow centre, and about 300 abroad. Besides these four directorates, there are also four directions which undertake the same duties. These directions do not form parts of directorates but are answerable to the first deputy chief. The first GRU direction carries out agent intelligence in the Moscow area and it has its influential representatives in all Soviet official institutions used by the GRU as cover: the Ministry of Foreign Affairs, the Ministry of External Trade, Aeroflot, the Merchant Navy, the Academy of Sciences and so forth. These representatives fit their young officers into slots in the institution serving as cover and guarantee their smooth progress in their future activities. In addition some GRU officers, on their return from overseas, continue to work in their covering organisation and not in the head office. Using these officers, the first direction recruits foreign military attachés, members of military delegations, businessmen and representatives of aviation and steamship companies. The second direction carries out agent intelligence in the area of East and West Berlin, a gigantic organisation which again does not form part of a directorate. The third direction is concerned with agent intelligence in national liberation movements and terrorist organisations. Its favourite child until recently was the Palestine Liberation Organisation. The fourth department carries out agent intelligence work from Cuban territory against many countries, including the United States. In many respects the fourth direction duplicates the activity of the second directorate. It has unlimited power in the ranks of the Cuban intelligence service and with its help actively penetrates and endeavours to direct the activities of unaligned movements.

The GRU adheres to a different principle in running its illegals from the principle adopted by the KGB. Among its procurement organs there is no separate unit for directing illegals, and the GRU does not consider such a unit necessary. Each of the directorate heads and several of the direction heads have under their command sections of illegals. This permits them to run illegals and residencies under cover at the same time in the territories of groups of countries or entire continents. The directorate or direction head may at any moment use his illegals for carrying out a secret check of the undercover residencies. The first deputy to the chief of the GRU also has an analogous section under his command. Naturally, he has very high-quality illegals. The first deputy may use his own illegals for secret checks on undercover residencies, and also the illegals under the command of directorate and direction heads. Finally, the absolute cream of the illegals are run personally by the chief of the GRU through his own illegals section. He can use his illegals for the checking of everything and everybody, including illegals under the command of the first deputy.

There is a fifth GRU directorate, which is also concerned with procurement and controlled by the first deputy. However, its functions differ from those on the four directorates and four directions listed above. The fifth directorate does not carry out independent agent intelligence work but directs the activities of the intelligence directorates of military districts, groups of forces and fleets. This directorate is a kind of controller of vassals. Directly under its control are twenty intelligence directorates belonging to the military districts, groups of forces and fleet

2. GRU: information-gathering

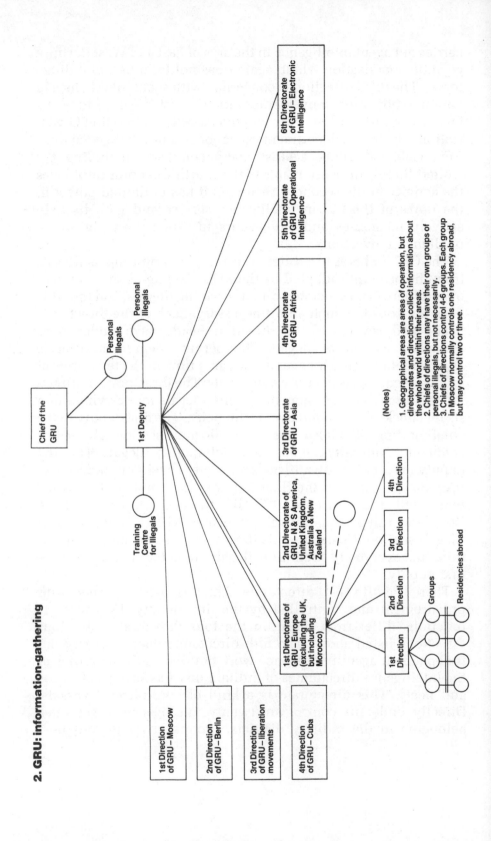

Chief of the GRU

1st Deputy

Personal Illegals

Personal Illegals

Training Centre for Illegals

3rd Directorate of GRU – Asia

2nd Directorate of GRU – N & S America, United Kingdom, Australia & New Zealand

1st Directorate of GRU – Europe (excluding the UK, but including Morocco)

4th Directorate of GRU – Africa

5th Directorate of GRU – Operational Intelligence

6th Directorate of GRU – Electronic Intelligence

1st Direction of GRU – Moscow

2nd Direction of GRU – Berlin

3rd Direction of GRU – liberation movements

4th Direction of GRU – Cuba

1st Direction

2nd Direction

3rd Direction

4th Direction

Groups

Residencies abroad

(Notes)

1. Geographical areas are areas of operation, but directorates and directions collect information about the whole world within their areas.
2. Chiefs of directions may have their own groups of personal illegals, but not necessarily.
3. Chiefs of directions control 4-6 groups. Each group in Moscow normally controls one residency abroad, but may control two or three.

intelligence, the latter having in its turn four more fleet intelligence directorates beneath it. The number of secret agents and diversionary agents ultimately controlled by the fifth directorate exceeds the number of all the agents controlled by the first four directorates and four directions, and these agents operate on all the same territories where illegals, undercover residencies and agents of the above-mentioned directorates and departments operate. With their help the first deputy, or indeed the chief himself, may secretly check on the activities of his directorate. This arrangement works in reverse too: with the help of agents of the first four directorates and four directions he can check the activities of the secret agents of military districts, fleets and groups of forces.

In addition to the proliferation of units outlined above, there are two more GRU directorates which are concerned with the procurement of information: the sixth directorate and the cosmic intelligence directorate. These directorates procure and partly process information, but they do not go in for agent intelligence, so they are not considered as purely procurement directorates and are not subordinate to the first deputy chief of the GRU. The chiefs of both these directorates answer to the chief of the GRU and are his deputies, but not first deputies.

The GRU sixth directorate is concerned with electronic intelligence. For this purpose its officers are posted to undercover residencies in the capitals of foreign states and there form groups which intercept and decipher transmissions on governmental and military networks. There are also many regiments of electronic intelligence on the territories of the Eastern bloc and Soviet Union, and these are integral parts of the sixth directorate. Furthermore, this directorate controls the electronic intelligence services of the military districts, groups of forces and fleets which in their turn have their own regiments, special ships, aircraft and helicopters for electronic espionage. The electronic espionage services of each military district, group and fleet correspondingly control similar services in the armies and flotillas, and these in their turn control those of the divisions. And so it goes on. All the information acquired from the electronic companies of divisions, electronic battalions of armies, regiments of military districts and groups of forces and spy ships of the fleet, is collected in the sixth directorate and analysed there.

The GRU cosmic intelligence directorate is no less powerful. It has its own cosmodromes, a number of research institutes, a co-ordinating computer centre and huge resources. It works out the technical details for spy satellites independently and prepares them in its own works. The Soviet Union has sent into orbit more than 2,000 cosmic objects for different purposes, and one in three of them belongs to the GRU. The vast majority of Soviet cosmonauts, with the exception of those who undertake only demonstration flights, work for half their time in space in the interests of the GRU. The KGB lies far behind the GRU in this respect.

Chapter Ten

Fleet Intelligence

The GRU fifth directorate directs twenty intelligence directorates of military districts and groups of forces directly, and four intelligence directorates of fleets co-ordinated by an organisation known as fleet intelligence. Fleet intelligence was introduced because each military district and group of forces has a very strictly defined sphere of responsibility in time of war, whereas the ships of the four Soviet fleets operate in widely scattered areas of the world's oceans and each ship must continuously have full information on the enemy. The chief of fleet intelligence comes under the GRU chief as a deputy, and he controls the four intelligence directorates of naval staff – Northern, Pacific, Black Sea and Baltic – and the fleet cosmic intelligence directorate and information service. In his day-to-day activities he is under the orders of the GRU fifth directorate.

Fleet intelligence directorates have a structure similar to that of the directorates of military districts. There are small differences caused by maritime factors, which for our purposes are insignificant, and the fleet intelligence directorates together with those belonging to military districts will be examined in detail in Part II under the heading of 'Operational Intelligence'.

The GRU chief has at his disposal two independent cosmic intelligence services. One is beneath him directly, the GRU cosmic intelligence directorate, and the other through the chief of fleet intelligence. The Soviet High Command quite reasonably considers that, bearing in mind the tasks to be fulfilled, the fleet must have its own cosmic intelligence service. This of course does not exclude the GRU chief controlling his own cosmic intelligence service with the help of the other and vice-versa. Considering that not only the GRU cosmic intelligence service, but also that of the fleets has its own spy satellites, we may say that out of all the satellites put into orbit by the Soviet Union, about half are directly or indirectly subordinated to the GRU.

Chapter Eleven

The GRU Processing Organs

The GRU processing organs are sometimes called the information service or more frequently simply 'information'. The chief of information has the rank of colonel-general and is a deputy to the GRU chief. The following are under his control:

  i   the information command point;
 ii   six information directorates;
iii   the institute of information;
 iv   the information services of fleet intelligence;
  v   the information services of intelligence directorates of military districts and groups;
 vi   all the organisations of military intelligence listed below which are concerned with the processing of secret material acquired.

The information command point is second only to the GRU central command point. It receives all intelligence material coming from illegals, undercover residencies, agents, from cosmic and electronic intelligence and also from the intelligence directorates of military districts, fleets, groups of forces, and from the military intelligence services of the satellite countries. It has full power to ask any resident, agent or illegal, in fact any source of intelligence information, to give more precise details or to re-check information submitted. The information command point works without breaks, without days off, without holidays. It carries out all preliminary processing of all the material submitted; each morning at six o'clock it publishes a top secret 'Intelligence Summary' destined for members of the Politburo and the higher military command, and in the morning all material which has come to hand during the previous twenty-four hours is transmitted to the informational directorates of the GRU for detailed analysis.

In all, there are six directorates plus the information institute on the strength of the information service. The numbering begins of course with the seventh directorate which is concerned with a study of NATO in all its aspects. The directorate consists of six departments, each of which consists of sections. Each department and each section carries responsibility for the study of individual trends or aspects of NATO activities. The eighth directorate carries out studies of individual countries worldwide, irrespective of whether that country belongs to NATO or not. Special attention is paid to questions of political structure, armed forces and economies, and special emphasis is put on a study of the personal activities of statesmen and military leaders. The ninth directorate studies military technology. It is very tightly connected with the Soviet design offices and with the armaments industry as a whole. It is the only link between the Soviet armaments factories copying foreign weapons and the residents of Soviet intelligence who obtain the necessary secrets. The tenth directorate studies military economics worldwide, carefully watching arms sales, studying production and technological developments, strategic resources and vulnerable points. The idea of an oil embargo first saw the light of day in this directorate as a suggestion in the 'Locomotive Report' of 1954, when it was pointed out that, to wreck the 'locomotive of capitalism' it was not necessary to smash the engine, only to deprive it of a crucial ingredient. Immediately after this the Soviet penetration of the Arab nations began. Happily this stunning idea of the tenth directorate has not as yet been put into practice. The eleventh studies strategic concepts and strategic nuclear forces of all countries who possess such capabilities, or may in the future possess them. This directorate carefully monitors any signs of increased activity, any change in emphasis in the activities of strategic nuclear forces in any region of the globe. The officers of this directorate form the backbone of Soviet delegations to the SALT talks. Unfortunately we do not possess reliable information on the activities of the twelfth directorate.

The gigantic information institute functions independently of the directorates. It is controlled by the chief of information but operates outside the walls of the GRU. As opposed to the directorates, which base their analyses of the situation exclusively on secret documents obtained by agent, electronic and cosmic intelligence, the institute studies overt sources: the press, radio and television. The Western press is a veritable treasure house for Soviet intelligence.

The activity of each information directorate in many respects duplicates the activity of its neighbour directorates. The advantage of such a set-up is that it prevents a one-sided view and a subjective approach to problems. Directorates and sections look at problems in a narrow, parochial manner, giving their opinions not on the whole question but only on a part. A unified opinion is worked out by the head of information with the help of his best experts and the command point. Many reports from the procurement organs of the GRU are analysed simultaneously by several or even by all units of the information at the same time. Let us suppose, for example, that a case officer belonging to an undercover residency receives a short verbal report from an agent to the effect that a new jet fighter is in the process of being developed in the United States and no official announcement has as yet been made. Immediately after the meeting with the agent the case officer would send an enciphered telegram, one brief sentence, to Moscow. But the information command point has no other report on this question, nor any evidence to support it. The report would be published in the 'Intelligence Summary' under the heading 'unchecked and unconfirmed report'. The next morning all members of the Politburo and the higher military command would receive the volume printed during the night. At the same time all branches of information would be studying the report. The seventh directorate, trying to put itself in the shoes of NATO leaders, would endeavour to calculate what present and future value this fighter would have for NATO and, if it were really to be taken into service, how it would affect the balance of power in Europe and in the world. The question of which country of the United States' allies would be likely to buy such an aircraft would also be studied. Units of the seventh directorate would immediately start searching their archives for information on what NATO leaders have said about the future development of aviation. Simultaneously with this the eighth directorate responsible for individual countries including US studies would thoroughly research the question as to who insisted on the decision to develop a new aircraft; what forces in the country might come out against such a decision; which aviation companies might be drawn into the development of the aircraft by tendering for the contract; who would be likely to win and who to lose. The ninth directorate, on the basis of an analysis of the latest American achievements in the sphere of engine building, aerodynamics, aviation electronics, might be able to foretell the basic technical parameters of the aircraft. The tenth directorate would unerringly tell, on the basis of an analysis of military orders, military budgets and the budgets of the country's main corporations, which aviation companies would actually be involved and to what extent. The eleventh directorate would study the problem from the angle of the aircraft's potential use as a carrier of nuclear weapons. It would be able to draw conclusions without knowing very much about the new aircraft, simply on the evidence of existing carriers of atomic weapons, their replacement in service, the quantity of nuclear weapons and plans for their utilisation. At the same time, the information institute would call up all overt publications which might have some bearing on the problem and present its own opinion to the information command point. And all residents, illegals, independently operating agents, intelligence directorates of military districts, fleets and army groups would receive appropriate orders to increase their activity with regard to the question. Such an order would also be received by the 'younger brothers'. By the evening reports of all the branches would be collected at the command point and be printed that night in the routine 'Intelligence Summary', amongst hundreds of similar reports already confirmed.

The GRU lays great stress on questions of training specialists for the information directorates. Alongside professional intelligence officers work the best specialists from a wide range of scientific, technical and industrial fields. The GRU has the right to co-opt any specialist from cosmic research or atomic energy, microbiology or computer technology, strategic planning or international relations. Such a right was accorded to the GRU by the Central Committee on the principle that it is better for the Soviet Union to be in the know about the most modern achievements of the United States, Japan, Great Britain, France and the Federal Republic of Germany than to work out its own. In conformity with this the GRU, during the most dramatic moments of the space race of the sixties, unceremoniously co-opted the leading Soviet specialists in the field of piloted cosmic flights and, with their help, monitored every step of the Americans' progress. It is evident that every Soviet programme was based on an American model, but launched days or even months before the Americans carried out theirs. As a result every record, including the first orbital flight, the first multi-seater spaceship, the first entry into outer space went to the Soviet Union. This state of affairs continued right up to the time when the adventurism of the Soviet programme produced a series of tragic accidents.

The information directorates of the GRU have at their disposal the highest quality electronic equipment produced by the best American firms, and the GRU leadership, not without reason, considers that the technical equipment of the processing organs of the GRU is vastly superior to that of comparable units within the CIA – in spite of the fact that some Western specialists have said that the GRU information service is not as effective as it should be. They base this on two facts: that in 1941 the GRU had all the data on the forthcoming German invasion but was unable to evaluate correctly the information it had, and secondly, that much of the intelligence material was reported to the higher command in a 'grey' unprocessed state. It is impossible to deny either of these facts, although one may complain that they belong to past history and not the present. If the GRU information service is truly less effective than it should be, the answer lies in the communist system itself. General Golikov did possess detailed German plans for the invasion, but Stalin was not of a mind to believe them. Two years before, he had twice liquidated the whole staff of Soviet military intelligence from the chief of the GRU downwards. So what more was Golikov to do? Thirteen years later, the new chief of the GRU, General Shtemyenko, found the solution. He ordered the publication of an intelligence summary each night, which would include 'grey', unprocessed information and unsubstantiated data. In this way the gallant general implied that 'this is not my opinion, it is the opinion of my residents'. The GRU chief and the head of information would only give their own opinion twenty-four hours later in the next issue of the summary. (This stroke of genius on the part of the GRU was immediately adopted by the KGB too, which in the same way began to print 'grey' information each night and save its judgements for the following day.)

In a totalitarian state, every lower level is completely dependent on its superior, and there is no organ which can defend it from the caprices of its superior. This is the very essence of the Soviet Union, and this is why it is necessary for the leaders of Soviet intelligence to have recourse to such cunning. The system has been well-tried up to the present time and serves as a kind of lightning conductor. The chief of the GRU camouflages his own opinion, always adopting the position adopted by the general secretary of the Party at a given moment, and at the same time he is able to present the developing situation to the leadership in a most objective way, thus transferring all responsibility from his shoulders to the shoulders of his subordinates. The overseas intelligence organs, separated by thousands of kilometres from Moscow, cannot possibly know what opinion their rulers hold at a given moment. They are therefore forced to give simply objective material which can be directly reported to the higher command. Only in this way can the intelligence leadership exert any influence on its stubborn masters when the latter do not wish to listen to any opinion which contradicts their own.

But the totalitarian system still exerts a crushing influence on all branches of society, including the intelligence services. Nobody has the right to object to, or contradict, the supreme command. Thus it was under Lenin and Stalin and Kruschev and Brezhnev, and thus it will be in the future. Should the supreme command have an incorrect view of things, then no intelligence or information service can convince it otherwise; it does not dare. Nor does first-class American equipment help, nor the very best specialists. It is not the fault of the intelligence services, it is the system's fault. In cases where the supreme command is frankly deluded, as Stalin was in 1941, intelligence has absolutely no chance of influencing him and its effectiveness at that moment is nil.

However, it is not always like that. If the desires of the dictator and his intelligence service coincide, then the latter's effectiveness grows many times greater. In this case, the totalitarian system is not a brake but an accelerator. The dictator does not care at all for moral sides of a question. He is not at all answerable before society for his actions; he fears no opposition or discussion; and he is able to supply his intelligence service with any amount of money, even at a moment when the country is suffering from hunger. The GRU has carried out its most brilliant operations at exactly such moments, when the opinions of the dictator and the intelligence service coincided. And the information service has played a first-class role on these occasions.

Let us consider one example. During the Second World War a section of the tenth directorate (economics and strategic resources) was studying the trends in the exchange of precious metals in the United States. The specialists were surprised that an unexpectedly large amount of silver was allocated 'for scientific research'. Never before, either in America or in any other country, had such a large amount of silver been spent for the needs of research. There was a war going on and the specialists reasonably supposed that the research was military. The GRU information analysed all the fields of military research known to it, but not one of them required the expenditure of so much silver. The second reasonable assumption by the GRU was that it was some new field of research concerning the creation of a new type of weapon. Every information unit was brought to bear on the study of this strange phenomenon. Further analysis showed that all publications dealing with atomic physics had been suppressed in the United States and that all atomic scientists, fugitives from occupied Europe, had at the same time disappeared without trace from the scientific horizon. A week later the GRU presented to Stalin a detailed report on developments in the USA of atomic weapons. It was a report which had been compiled on the basis of only one unconfirmed fact, but its contents left no room for doubt about the correctness of the deductions it made. Stalin was delighted with the report: the rest is well known.

Chapter Twelve

Support Services

All GRU organs which are not directly concerned with the provision or processing of intelligence material are considered as support services. It is not possible for us to examine all of these, but we will simply take briefly the most important of them.

The Political Department is concerned with the ideological monitoring of all GRU personnel. The military rank of the head of the political department is lieutenant-general and again he is a deputy to the GRU chief. As opposed to any other political departments the GRU political department is made up not of party officials but of professional intelligence officers. There are also several other differences. All political directorates and departments of the Soviet Army are subordinated to the chief political directorate of the Soviet Army, which is at the same time one of the Central Committee departments. The GRU political department, however, is subordinated directly to the Central Committee administrative department. The political department of the GRU has considerable weight in Moscow, especially as regards staff movements, but it has no right to interfere in intelligence work. It exerts practically no influence on the activities of overseas branches of the GRU. Overseas the residents are personally responsible for the ideological monitoring of their officers.

The Personnel Directorate is directly beneath the chief of the GRU. The head of the directorate, a lieutenant-general, is also a deputy to the chief of the GRU. The directorate is staffed only by intelligence officers who, in common with officers of the procurement and processing organs, the political department and other branches of the GRU, regularly go abroad for a period of several years and then return to work at domestic postings.

The personnel directorate has exceptional influence both in the GRU and outside. It directs the movements of all officers, not only inside the GRU, but in a number of satellites, in fleet intelligence, intelligence directorates of military districts and groups of forces too, and also in the intelligence services of Eastern bloc countries.

The Operational/Technical Directorate is concerned with the development and production of all espionage equipment and apparatus. Within its dominion fall several scientific research institutes and specialised undertakings. On the orders of the procurement organs the directorate prepares equipment for secret writing and micro-photography, several kinds of dead letter-box, radio appliances, eavesdropping material, armaments and poisons, to name but a few. Its head is a lieutenant-general, although he is not classed officially as a deputy.

The Administrative/Technical Directorate is in charge of foreign currencies and other items of value, gold and diamonds, for example. This directorate is the currency middle-man between the military industrial commission and the operational users. It controls all the currency resources of the GRU and also carries out secret speculative operations on the international market. Possessed of colossal currency resources, it frequently uses them in order to exert secret pressure on individual businessmen, statesmen and sometimes even on whole governments. No less important, it is responsible for the growth of capital belonging to the GRU and for the acquisition of 'clean' currency.

The Communications Directorate deals with the organisation of radio and other communication between the GRU and its overseas units. Needless to say, it controls several powerful reception and transmission centres of its own, but should the need arise to secure special channels of communication, in case of a worsening of operational conditions, for example, then it can make use of the services of the cosmic intelligence directorate, communicating with illegals and agents by means of GRU satellites.

The Financial Department: unlike the administrative/technical directorate, the financial department deals only with Soviet money, not with foreign currency. The financial department carries out legal financial operations in the Soviet Union.

The First GRU Department (Passport) studies passport regulations worldwide. In the pursuit of this esoteric duty it has the greatest collection in the world of passports, identity cards, driving licences, military documents, passes, police documents, railway, air and sea tickets. The department keeps maps of many thousands of frontier posts, customs and police posts, and so on. The department can at any moment say what documents are required at any given control point in the world, what sort of questions are asked, and what stamps are to be put on the passports and other documents. Within a few hours, it can forge the passport of any country to conform with the latest changes in the passport and visa regulations of that country, having at its disposal hundreds of thousands of blanks for new passports, identity cards and driving licences for every country in the world. In my experience, the preparation of the papers which will preserve one's true identity can be done in a very short time.

The Eighth GRU Department is the most secret of all the top secret units of the GRU. The eighth department possesses all the GRU's secrets. It is here that the enciphering and deciphering of all incoming and outgoing documents is carried out.

The Archives Department is possibly the most interesting of all the departments. In its cellars are millions of personal details and files on illegals, domestic officers, undercover residencies, successful recruitment of foreigners (and unsuccessful ones), material on everyone from statesmen and army heads to prostitutes and homosexuals and designers of rockets and submarines. In every file lies the fate of an individual, in every file there is an unwritten novel.

Part Two

Chapter One

Illegals

We can define an illegal as an officer of strategic intelligence performing the tasks of the Centre on the territory of a foreign state, who passes himself off as a foreigner but not as a Soviet citizen. Illegals are frequently confused with agents, but these are completely different things. The crucial difference is that the agent is an inhabitant of a foreign country who has been recruited by, and works in the interest of, Soviet intelligence, whereas an illegal is first and foremost a Soviet officer passing himself off as a foreigner. Sometimes some of the most valuable and deserving agents receive Soviet citizenship as an incentive and are awarded the rank of an officer of the GRU or the KGB, but even so, an agent remains an agent. However, in the occasional case when a foreigner has been recruited by Soviet intelligence and for some reason or other changes his appearance or name and continues his activities with *false* documents, then he is called an illegal agent.

Both the GRU and the KGB have their own illegal networks, but these are completely independent one from the other. Each organisation selects, trains, prepares, deploys and utilises its illegals as it sees fit. In the same way each organisation separately works out principles, methods of work and technical details of the illegal system separately. The system of running illegals is entirely different in the two services. In the KGB there is a special directorate of illegal activities. In the GRU, all illegals are trained in a training centre under the leadership of Lieutenant-General V. T. Guryenko. After their training, the illegals are put at the disposal of the heads of the four geographical directorates and are controlled personally by them. Thus each directorate head supervises a number of directions and separately a group of illegals. In order to help him, the directorate head can call on a small group of advisers consisting in the main of former illegals (though not 'blown' ones) who are ready at any moment, using false papers, to go to the target country and 'fine-tune' and help the activities of the illegal networks. Directorate heads themselves frequently travel abroad for the same reasons. A number of the more important illegals are directly controlled by the first deputy head of the GRU, and there is a cream who are under the personal supervision of the head of the GRU. Thus both one and the other have small groups consisting of the most experienced and successful illegals who have returned from abroad and who exercise supervision over the daily running of the illegals. If a young illegal begins to acquire really interesting information he is transferred from the control of the head of a directorate to that of the first deputy or, in the case of even greater success, to that of the head of the GRU himself. This is, of course, a very high honour, granted only to those who return information of a very high calibre – unprecedented or highly classified material which produces an intelligence breakthrough. Equally an illegal may be demoted for failing to produce the goods. In certain cases his grade may fall below that which is supervised by the head of a directorate and he will be supervised only by the head of a direction. This is a very critical stage for the illegal, although he may not even be able to guess that it has happened. If he is demoted to direction head level – and he is, of course, not informed about this – the next step could well be a recall to the Soviet Union, regarded by all intelligence personnel as the direst form of punishment. Recall to the Soviet Union is a particularly effective measure against any Soviet citizen serving abroad. It is all the same to them whether they are in Paris or in Pnom Penh. The only important thing is that they should not be in the Soviet Union, and transfer to the Soviet Union, even on promotion, is regarded as the tragedy of a lifetime.

The selection of potential illegals is carried out by each of the four geographical directorates independently. Candidates are selected on the basis of future requirements. In basic terms, officers of the Soviet Army and Navy are used who as yet may know nothing about the GRU. Sometimes experienced officers of the GRU are used, those who have completed the Military-Diplomatic Academy and have already worked in intelligence or in the information processing departments. Sometimes the GRU will select for illegal activities young Soviet citizens, mainly those who have completed linguistic courses in higher education.

Higher education is an essential requirement, therefore the minimum age at which a recruit will begin his training is 21 to 23 years.

Although General Guryenko's organisation is called the 'Training Centre', not one Soviet illegal who has defected has ever been able to say exactly where it is. The name Training Centre seems simply to reflect the existence of one organisation occupied with one task. Either the organisation is constantly on the move, or a secluded little place is selected for each individual trainee, normally in the Moscow area where there are great numbers of dachas. The dachas for the training of illegals are well concealed among other governmental buildings, where outsiders are not to be seen on the streets and unnecessary questions are not asked, but gentlemen of sporting appearance may be seen walking in pairs in the quiet shady avenues. The dacha provides an ideally isolated territory for training. In addition to the candidate and his family, two or three instructors also live in the dacha where they can immerse him completely and supervise him very carefully all the time. His wife is also trained but the children lead normal lives and will be held eventually as hostages. The internal fittings of the dacha are prepared very thoroughly and carefully. From the first day the candidate becomes accustomed to the circumstances in which he will be living and working probably for many long years. In this connection he wears the clothes and shoes, and eats the food, even smokes cigarettes and uses razor blades procured from overseas. In each room a tape recorder is installed which runs twenty-four hours a day while he is occupying the dacha. These tape recorders continuously broadcast news from the radio programmes of his target country. From the first day of his training he is supplied with the majority of papers and magazines. He sees many films and descriptions on video tapes of television broadcasts. The instructors, for the most part former illegals, read the same papers and listen to the same radio programmes and spend their time asking their pupil the most difficult questions imaginable with regard to what has been read. It is quite obvious that after a number of years of such training, the future illegal knows by heart the composition of every football team, the hours of work of every restaurant and nightclub, the weather forecasts and everything that is going on in the realm of gossip as well as current affairs, in a country where he has never been in his life. The instructional programme is tailor-made for each trainee, giving due consideration to his knowledge, character and the tasks which he will be called upon to perform in the future. Attention is obviously paid to the study of the language of the target country, to working methods and to a cover story.

Often, the illegal's wife also undergoes training. She as a rule works as the radio operator. The posting of a husband and wife together, leaving their children behind as hostages, is a very frequent occurrence. It is considered that maternal feelings are much the stronger and, with the wife posted, hostages are that much more effective. Perhaps more surprisingly, the wife also acts as a control for the GRU on her husband. She scrutinises his behaviour and sometimes may warn the GRU about his excessive interest in women or alcohol. On their return to the Soviet Union, husband and wife are subjected to a detailed individual de-briefing on all aspects of their life abroad. If the husband and wife have decided to keep something secret from the GRU, their stories will eventually differ.

After as much as three or four years of intensive training, the illegal passes a state commission of top GRU and Central Committee personnel, and goes abroad. Usually his journey to the target country is effected through a number of intermediary countries. For example, a journey to the USA would go from the Soviet Union to Hungary to Yugoslavia to Cyprus, Kuwait, Hong Kong and Hawaii. At each stage, or most of them, he destroys documents with which he has entered the country and goes on under new documentation which has been prepared for him, either by other illegals or by the residencies under cover. The illegal will find these documents in a reserved hotel or a steam-ship cabin or in a letter through the post. At each stage he goes on to another cover story, becoming another man. He may have to live in one place for some months and study it so he can use his knowledge of the country in future cover stories. He does not stop over at all in some of the countries, only using his visit to cover his tracks. After some months he arrives at the country where he is to work. The first thing he does is to visit the city where he is supposed to have been born, gone to school, and married. He gets a job and works for a time, after which he returns to the Soviet Union, having finished the second stage of his training – the illegal probationary period abroad. This probationary period is divided as a rule into one or two years, after which the third stage begins. On the basis of the experience he has gained, and the shortcomings which have come to light in the training, the illegal and his instructors work out a programme of training for a period which lasts another one or two years. After this he again undergoes state examinations, at which the head of the GRU or his first deputy have to be present. Then the illegal is placed at the disposal of one of the heads of directorates and again commences the operation for his roundabout journey to the target country. For operational purposes (though not for instructional purposes) much use is made of Finland as a window to the West. In the course of his operational journey, the illegal's stay in one of the intermediate countries may continue for several years. This stage goes by the name of the 'intermediate legalisation'. To take the case of an illegal whose target destination is Washington: he might pretend to be a refugee from Hungary escaped in 1956; this would mean periods of residence in Hungary to begin with, then Austria and Germany before he arrives finally in America. An eventual French illegal would be likely to make the journey via Armenia and Lebanon. Both would consolidate their nationality every step of the way. In the course of the 'intermediate legalisation', the illegal endeavours to acquire as many friends as possible, to go to work, to get hold of genuine papers and character and work references. At the end of these years of preparation, he at last appears in the country where he is to spend so many more years endeavouring to do it as much harm as possible.

The minimum age of an illegal clearly cannot be less than twenty-seven to twenty-nine, but usually he is older, on average about forty. This age suits the GRU very well for a number of reasons. A man of forty has a balanced, conservative approach to life. The stormy passions of youth have disappeared and he is less inclined to take ill-considered decisions, especially if he ever suffers the dilemma of whether to continue working or to go to the police. His children are sufficiently old to be able to live without their parents in the complete care of the GRU, but not old enough to live independently, and so they are ideal hostages. And in the event of mobilisation in the target country, he may well be able to avoid being called up for the army which would mean the breaking-off of relations and an end to his active working life.

On his arrival at his objective, the illegal sets about basic

79

legalisation. He has been provided with good papers by the best forgers of the GRU on genuine blank passports. At the same time he is extremely vulnerable if he is not registered with the police or the tax departments. Any check may give him away and for this reason he endeavours to change jobs and places of work often to get his name onto as many company lists as he can and to acquire character references signed by real people. The ideal solution is for him to obtain new documentation from the police department under some pretext or another. Often he will marry another agent (who may already be his wife); she will then be given a genuine passport, and he will 'lose' his false one to have it replaced with a real one on the production of his wife's genuine document. The acquisition of a driving licence, credit cards, membership documents of clubs and associations are a vital element in 'legalising' the status of an illegal.

A vital role in the lives of illegals is played by cover stories, in other words concocted life stories. The basic or ground cover story is created on the basis of real events in the life of the illegal, only changing a few details. He keeps the date of his birth but of course changes the place of his birth. The dates of birth of his parents and relatives are also accurately recorded, usually along with the professions of his parents, dates of weddings and other details. The illegal is thus not telling an out-and-out lie but only a half-truth. He will not bat an eyelid when he tells you that his father served all his life in the army. The only thing is that he will not tell you in which army he served.

There is also the emergency cover story, which is the last line of defence of the illegal on having been arrested by the police. As its name suggests, this cover story is only to be used as a last resort when the illegal perceives that the police no longer believe his basic cover story. Designed to be used only when the illegal is in the hands of the police department, it is concocted in such a way that the details it gives should be impossible to check. For example, one illegal was arrested by the police while he was trying to obtain a new driving licence because a mistake had been found in his old one. He was subjected to questioning, as a result of which his basic cover story was found to be inaccurate. Then he went over to his emergency cover story and informed the police that he was a Polish criminal who had escaped from prison and bought a passport on the black market. During this time the GRU, not having received from the illegal his routine communications, informed the Polish authorities about the 'criminal'. The Poles published photographs of the criminal and applied to a number of countries for his extradition. However strange it may seem, the police believed the story and handed him over to the Polish Consul. It would have been easy to break the emergency cover story, if the police had only thought to invite a real Polish immigrant for a ten-minute chat with his supposed fellow countryman. Of course he would not have known more than ten words of the language. But for the police it was sufficient that he spoke their language and did not object to being handed over to the Polish Consul.

No less important than the cover story is the cover or the place of work and the type of employment which the illegal takes up in his life overseas. Soviet propaganda paints a grave picture of the intelligence officer playing the role of a colonel in the enemy general staff. But this is pure disinformation. Such a cover is unacceptable to an illegal for a number of reasons. Firstly, he must keep himself away from counter-intelligence and the police. He must be a grey, inconspicuous 'man in the street' such as millions would hurry past without noticing. Any officer on any Western general staff is continuously under scrutiny. Secondly, he must be professional in his field. In the general staff he would be exposed almost immediately. Thirdly, for such a cover his legalisation would have to be unacceptably protracted. He would certainly be asked about the military schools and academies where he is supposed to have been, the regiments in which he has served, and his acquaintances among the officers and staff. Fourthly, an illegal needs plenty of time and opportunity to meet whoever he wants to meet. If a colonel on the general staff consorted with prostitutes, homosexuals, stockbrokers, atomic submarine workers and bootblacks – all those multifarious people he needs to cultivate – he would be exposed within forty-eight hours. Finally, and perhaps most importantly, the requirements of the GRU change with great rapidity. Today they are interested in documents from a certain department of the general staff and tomorrow from another. But our illegal is working in yet another department and all his attempts to have talks with officers of the first two departments have been met with a blank wall or cold suspicion. No, the kind of cover offered by such a role is neither feasible nor a great deal of use.

Much better for him to be an independent journalist like Richard Sorge, or an independent artist like Rudolph Abel, coming and going as he pleases. Today he is talking with the Prime Minister, tomorrow with prostitutes, the next day with professional killers and then with atomic weapon workers. If he doesn't want to work for three months, there is no problem. If he gets many thousands of dollars through the post, again no problem. It is part of his cover. There are better, of course. A garage owner, for example. He hires his staff and himself goes wherever he wants and for as long as he wants, or he stands at the window and takes the money. Thousands of people pass him every day – ballerinas and artists, senators and scientists – and colonels of the general staff. To one he gives money and instructions written in secret writing, from another he receives reports. For the basic task of the illegal is not himself to penetrate secret targets, but to recruit agents for this purpose. This is his *raison d'être*.

*

An illegal residency is an intelligence organisation comprising a minimum of two illegals, usually the resident and a wireless operator, and a small number of agents (at least one) working for them. We already know that illegals themselves, without agents, are not able to obtain anything. Gradually, as a result of recruiting new agents, the residency may increase in size. More illegals may be sent out to the resident, one of whom may become his assistant. The GRU considers it counter-productive to have large residencies. Five illegals and eight to ten agents are considered the maximum, but usually the residencies are much smaller than this. In cases where the recruitment of new agents has gone well the GRU prudently divides the residency in two parts. Thereafter any contact between the two new residencies is of course forbidden, so that if one residency is discovered the other does not suffer.

Chapter Two

The Undercover Residency

The undercover residency is one of the basic forms of intelligence set-up for the GRU abroad. (It should be remembered that the undercover residency and the illegal residency are completely separate entities.) In every country where official Soviet representation exists there is a GRU undercover residency. It exists in parallel with, and is analogous to, the KGB undercover residency. Thus every overseas Soviet colony is invisibly divided into three organisations: the 'clean ones', that is the genuine diplomats and correspondents, and the representatives of external trade, civil airlines, the merchant navy, and Intourist, headed by the ambassador; the undercover residency of the GRU; and the undercover residency of the KGB.

Very often, the 'clean' personnel make no distinction between the KGB and the GRU and call them both dirty, 'savages', 'Vikings' or 'neighbours'. The more enlightened staff, like for example the ambassador, his senior diplomats and the more observant people, understand the difference between the two organisations, dividing them up as close neighbours (the KGB), who continually meddle in the day-to-day affairs of each person in the colony, and distant neighbours who take absolutely no interest at all in the day-to-day life of the Soviet colony (the GRU).

For the GRU undercover residency lives a secluded and isolated life. It contains significantly fewer employees than either of the other organisations. Normally in Soviet colonies up to 40 per cent of the people may be considered in the 'clean' category. (This of course does not prevent the majority of them, to a greater or lesser extent, from co-operation with both the KGB and the GRU; but they are not to be considered as professional intelligence officers.) Up to 40 or 45 per cent are officers of the KGB and only 15 to 20 per cent, in rare cases up to 25 per cent, are officers of the GRU. This does not however mean that the intelligence potential of the GRU apparatus is less than that of the KGB. The larger part of the KGB personnel is occupied with questions of security, that is with the collection of compromising material on Soviet people, 'clean' people including the ambassador, and their own colleagues in the KGB who have contact with foreigners and frequently with officers of the GRU. Only a small proportion, in optimum cases half of the KGB personnel, are working against foreigners. The GRU, on the other hand, directs its entire potential against foreigners. When one adds to this the unequalled financial power of the GRU, vastly in excess of that of the KGB, it becomes clear why the most outstanding operations of Soviet intelligence have been mounted not by the KGB but by the GRU.

The minimum number of staff for any GRU undercover residency is two – the resident and a combined radio/cipher officer. Such a theoretical minimum exists also for the other organisations, the KGB and the Ministry of Foreign Affairs. Theoretically the Soviet colony in a very small country may consist of six people, three of whom, the ambassador and two residents, are diplomats, and the other three radio/cipher officers. Each of the three branches of the Soviet colony has its own enciphering machine and completely independent channel of communication with Moscow. Equally, each has its own boss in Moscow—the Minister of Foreign Affairs, the chairman of the KGB or the head of the GRU. Supreme arbitration between them can only be carried out in the Central Committee, which in its turn has an interest in fanning the flames of discord between the three organisations. The Central Committee has the right to recall any ambassador or resident and this same Central Committee has to decide questions as to which slots, and how many, should be accorded to each of the three organisations. This is a difficult task, as the Committee must not offend the KGB on questions of security, on the shadowing of its own diplomats above all, nor must it offend the GRU, for without the acquisition of data on present-day technology the quality of the Soviet Army would remain static. Finally it must not offend the 'clean ones'. They also must have a sufficient complement to serve as a screen for the dark activities of the two residencies.

This is why Soviet embassies, consulates, trade representations and so on grow and multiply and swell. As the residency grows, the resident acquires several deputies in place of the one he had at first. The number of radio/cipher officers increases. A technical services group is organised, an operational group, a tech-ops group, a radio monitoring station on the networks of the police and counter-intelligence. The number of operational officers engaged directly in recruiting and running agents increases. In the very biggest residencies of the GRU, such as that in New York, there may be from seventy to eighty officers. Medium-sized residencies like that in Rome would contain between thirty and forty officers. All officers on the staff of a residency are divided into three categories – operational staff, technical-operational staff and technical staff. The operational staff are those officers who are directly concerned with recruiting and running agents. In the operational staff are included residents, deputy residents and operational officers. To the technical-operations staff belong those officers who are directly concerned with and responsible for the production of intelligence, but who do not have personal contact with agents, nor often with foreigners at all. These are radio/cipher officers, officers of the technical services and operational technical services and the operators of the radio monitoring post. To the technical staff belong chauffeurs, guards and accountants.

The Resident
He is the senior representative of the GRU in any given place, and answerable only to the head of the GRU and the Central Committee. He is the boss of all GRU officers and has the right to send any of them, including his own deputies, out of the country immediately. In this case he does not even have to justify his decision, even in front of the head of the GRU and the Central Committee. The resident is completely responsible for security, both as regards the work of each of his individual officers and recruited agents, and the security of the residency as a whole. He is chosen from among the most experienced officers and as a rule must have a minimum of three to five years of successful work as an operational officer and three to five years as the deputy resident before his appointment. A resident in a large residency will hold the military rank of major-general, in medium and small residencies that of colonel. This does not mean that a lieutenant-colonel cannot be appointed resident, but then, according to the

GRU system, he will be paid a full colonel's or major-general's salary and, if he copes successfully, will have to fill posts commensurate with the higher rank. He is not afterwards permitted to return to a post ordinarily filled by a lieutenant-colonel.

The deputy resident serves as the resident's assistant and assumes his responsibilities when he is absent. He undertakes the duties given to him by the resident and carries on recruiting work in the same way as all other operational officers. Frequently a deputy resident heads teams of officers working in one or another specialised field. Sometimes the resident himself supervises the most experienced operational officers and the deputy residents the younger, less experienced officers. In some very large residencies, and also sometimes where there is great activity on the part of GRU illegals, there is a post called deputy resident for illegals. The undercover residency and the illegal residency are completely separate and the undercover residency has no idea how many illegals there are, or where or how they work. At the same time, on instructions from the Centre, the undercover residency continually gives them help and support, placing money and passports in dead-letter boxes, emptying dead-letter boxes for them, studying conditions and clarifying certain important questions. Very often the undercover residency is used to rescue illegals.

The military rank of any deputy resident is full colonel. At the same time the same rules apply as apply to residents. The deputy resident may be a lieutenant-colonel or even a major; however, from the administrative and financial points of view he is a full colonel with full rights.

The Operational Officer
This is a GRU officer who carries out the recruitment of agents, runs them and through them receives or acquires the secret documents and samples of weaponry and military technology. Every operational officer from the moment of his arrival in the country is obliged to recruit a minimum of one agent, as well as often having to take charge of one or two other secret agents who have previously been recruited by his predecessors. He must keep these agents and increase their productivity. An identical burden is placed on the deputy resident at the same time as he is fulfilling the obligations of a deputy. This system is applied in all small

residencies. In medium-sized residencies, the resident himself may take a direct interest in recruitment or not as he wishes. The residents of very large residencies are exempted from personal recruitment.

Alongside his recruitment work, the operational officer carries on with the acquisition of intelligence material by all possible means. He converses with foreigners, travels around the country and reads the press avidly. However, the GRU's over-riding view is that recruitment work is the most important part of an officer's duty, and it calls it number one (in addition to certain other colloquial words). All other work – support and the performing of operations for others, however important – is known as zero. One may be added to zero if a 'zero' agent manages to recruit a foreigner, in which case he becomes a '10', which is clearly the best number to be. For this reason an operational officer who has been abroad for three years and not recruited a single agent, even if he has achieved outstanding success in collecting the most interesting intelligence material, is considered to be idle. According to the standards of the GRU, he has sat for three years doing absolutely nothing and therefore hardly merits consideration for another overseas posting.

The military rank of an operational officer is lieutenant-colonel or colonel but in practice he may be a major (as I was) or captain, or even a senior lieutenant. If he is successful in his recruitment work he stays on at this level receiving automatic promotion according to the length of time served. If he does not manage to recruit any agents, he is deprived of all his colonel's privileges and again becomes an ordinary senior lieutenant or captain and has to compete for promotion in the ordinary way, as automatic promotion is not granted to unsuccessful officers.

The military ranks prescribed for undercover residencies are also applicable for illegal residencies, with the sole difference that the illegal resident may be a major-general having many fewer people under his command than the resident of the undercover residency.

The Radio/Cipher Officer
Although he is an officer of technical operational staff, and his military rank is not usually higher than that of major, the radio/cipher officer is the second most important person in the resi-

dency. He is not only responsible for cipher matters, the storage and use of ciphers and cipher machines, but also for the transmission and reception of enciphered cables and the storage of all secret documentation in the residency. The radio/cipher officer possesses all the secrets of the residency and since he deciphers communications from Moscow he knows the news even earlier than the resident. Nobody, including the ambassador and the KGB resident, at any time or under any pretext has the right of access to his room. They do not even have the right to know the number and types of cipher machines installed there. These restrictions also apply to GRU deputy residents. Even during periods when the resident is away and the deputy resident is acting for him he does not have the right to go into the radio/cipher operator's room or to ask him any specific questions which have a bearing on his work. Only the resident may exercise any control over the cipher officer, and he pays for the privilege because the cipher officer is the only man in the residency who is entitled to communicate with Moscow without the knowledge of the resident. He can send a cable containing an adverse report about the resident of which the resident himself will know nothing. It is the duty of the cipher officer to exercise silent watch over the behaviour of the resident, and if there is any shortcoming he must report it. In small residencies, where there is only one radio/cipher officer, only the resident may replace him should he become incapacitated for any reason. If both the resident and the cipher officer should become incapacitated at the same time then the deputy resident and the whole residency will remain completely cut off from the Centre. Naturally the ambassador's and the KGB's channels of communication can be used, but only in order to inform the GRU in a very general way. It is natural therefore that great care is taken of cipher officers (this is just as true of the KGB as the GRU). Draconian living conditions are imposed on all cipher officers. They are only allowed to live in official Soviet embassy accommodation guarded around the clock. Neither the cipher officer nor his wife is allowed to leave the guarded territory independently or unaccompanied. They are at all times led by an officer who enjoys diplomatic immunity. Neither the officer nor his wife is allowed near places where foreigners are to be found. Even if these foreigners are Bulgarians or Mongolians and are on guarded territory belonging to a Soviet embassy, the restriction remains in force. The cipher officer is not allowed in the same room with them even though he may be silent and in the company of his resident. He and his family must have a diplomatic escort on their journey out from the Soviet Union and on their return. During the time of his assignment abroad, he is forbidden all leave. It is easy to see why cipher officers are not posted abroad for longer than two years.

Of course those cipher officers who have served their whole lives on the territory of the Soviet Union deeply envy those who have had postings abroad, no matter where; and those who have been abroad will give their right arms to get another posting abroad, no matter where – Calcutta, Shanghai or Beirut. They will agree to any conditions, any climate, any restrictions on their family lives, for they have learnt with their mother's milk the rule that overseas life is always better than in the Soviet Union.

Technical Services (TS) Officer

They are concerned with electronic intelligence from the premises of official Soviet premises, embassies, consulates, and so on. Basic targets are the telecommunications apparatus of the government, diplomatic wireless communications, and military channels of communication. By monitoring radio transmissions, secret and cipher, technical services groups not only obtain interesting information but also cover the system of governmental communications, subordination of the different components of the state and the military structure.

The military ranks of technical services officers are major and lieutenant-colonel.

Radio Monitoring Station Officers

In contradistinction to TS officers, these are concerned with monitoring the radio networks of the police and security services. The technical services and the radio monitoring station are two different groups, independent of each other, both controlled by the resident. The difference between them is that the technical services work in the interests of the Centre, trying to obtain state secrets, but the monitoring station works only in the interests of the residency trying to determine where in the city police activity is at its highest at a given moment and thus where operations may be mounted and where they should not be mounted. Groups for the study of operational conditions are made up of the most junior officers who will eventually become operational officers and be sent out on independent recruitment work. These are small groups who continually study the local press and police activities, endeavouring to obtain by means of isolated snippets a general picture of the police work in a given city and country. Besides their scanning of police reports for an ultimate overview, they also minutely study and analyse, for example, the numbers of police vehicles which appear in newspaper pictures or the surnames of police officers and detectives. Sometimes this painstaking work brings unexpected results. In one country a keen journalist on a small newspaper reported a police plan to install secret television cameras in order to survey the most highly populated parts of the city; this was enough for the GRU to become interested and to take corresponding measures. Within a month the GRU resident was able to say with conviction that he was fully informed with regard to the police system of control by television and this enabled the whole residency successfully to avoid traps laid for them for several years. The military ranks of officers of these groups are senior lieutenant and captain.

The Operational Technical Group
This is concerned with the repair and maintenance of photographic apparatus, photocopying equipment and the like. At the disposal of the group there are dead-letter boxes of all types, radio transmission stations, SW (secret writing) materials, microphotography and micropantography. The officers of this group are always on hand to give the necessary explanations to operational officers and to instruct them on the use of this or that instrument or method. These officers continually monitor television programmes and collect useful items on video tape, giving to Moscow material it could not get from any other source. The officers of the group, together with the officers of the group for the study of operational conditions, are widely used for the security of agent operations, the carrying out of counter-surveillance, signals organisation, dead-letter box operations and so on.

Technical Personnel
Only the very largest residencies contain technical personnel. Drivers are only allocated to residents who hold the rank of

general. However, many generals, in an effort to be indistinguishable from other diplomats, dispense with the services of drivers. The military rank of a driver is an ensign. However, sometimes an operational officer is to be found in the guise of a driver and he, of course, has a much superior rank. This is a widespread method of deception, for who would pay attention to a driver?

Some residencies, especially those in countries where attacks on the embassy cannot be excluded, have a staff of guards besides the KGB guards who are responsible for the external protection of the building. The GRU internal security guards consist of young Spetsnaz officers in the rank of lieutenant or senior lieutenant. The internal security guards of the residency may be deployed at the request of the resident in countries where KGB attempts to penetrate the GRU get out of hand. The internal security guards answer directly to the resident or his deputy. Naturally they do not take part in agent handling operations.

An accountant, in the rank of captain or major, is employed only in those residencies where the normal monthly budget exceeds one million dollars. In other cases the financial affairs are the concern of one of the deputy residents.

*

In our examination of the undercover residency, we have naturally to examine its cover, the official duties used by KGB and GRU officers to camouflage their secret activities. Without exaggeration it may be said that any official duty given to Soviet citizens abroad may be used to mask officers of intelligence organisations: as ambassadors and drivers, consuls and guards, dancers, writers, artists, simple tourists, guides and stewardesses, heads of delegations and simple section heads, UN employees and priests, intelligence officers conceal their true functions. Any person who has the right of official entry and exit from the Soviet Union may be used for intelligence tasks, and the vast majority of these are in fact only occupied in intelligence work. Some types of cover provide better possibilities, some worse. Some are used more by the GRU, some more by the KGB. Let us look at the basic ones.

The embassy is used to an equal extent by both organisations. Both residents and their deputies are in possession of massive

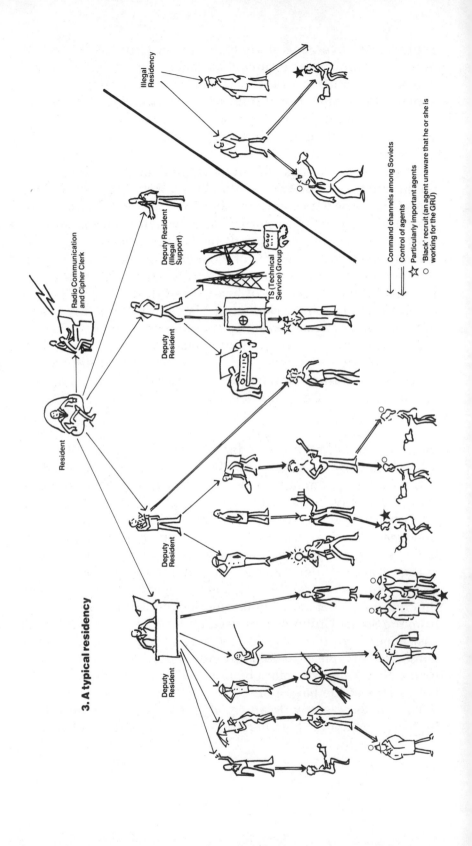

3. A typical residency

Resident

Radio Communication and Cipher Clerk

Deputy Resident (Illegal Support)

Deputy Resident

TS (Technical Service) Group

Deputy Resident

Deputy Resident

Illegal Residency

——— Command channels among Soviets

===== Control of agents

☆ Particularly important agents

○ 'Black' recruit (an agent unaware that he or she is working for the GRU) amounts of information which would expose them to an un-acceptably high risk of arrest. For this reason the KGB resident and his colleague from the GRU, and usually their deputies too, are bearers of diplomatic passports, that is, they work officially in the embassies. Other officers of both organisations give them-selves out as embassy diplomats too. They all prefer to concern themselves with technological and scientific questions, and ques-tions of transport and communications; they are rarely found in cultural sections. The consulate is entirely KGB. You will almost never find officers of the GRU there and only very rarely genuine diplomats. This is because all exit and entry from and to the Soviet Union is in the hands of the KGB. KGB officers in the consulate issue visas, and the frontier forces of the KGB then control them later on. Every aspect of immigration and of flight and defection has some connection with consular affairs, which therefore rank extremely high in the KGB's sphere of interest. So it follows that the percentage of KGB officers in consulates is unusually high, even by Soviet standards. (There do exist very rare instances of GRU officers working in consulates. The KGB only agrees to this on the grounds of practical considerations, and so that it should not appear to be too one-sided an organisation.)

Aeroflot, the Soviet civil airline, is the exclusive domain of the GRU. This can be explained by the fact that aviation technology is of extreme interest to the Soviet armaments industry, and there is huge scope for any Aeroflot employee to inform himself about the progress of the West: international exhibitions, meetings with representatives of the leading aviation and space corporations, perfectly justifiable meetings with representatives of firms pro-ducing aviation electronics, oils, lubricants, fuels, high-tension materials, heat isolators and aero-engines. Usually the firms which produce civil aircraft also produce military aircraft and rockets, and in this field lie the GRU's richest pickings. Happily, those officers whom the GRU selects at advanced aviation insti-tutes for work in Aeroflot do not need lengthy specialist instruc-tion. Sometimes Soviet military and civil aircraft have identical parts. KGB officers are only rarely employed at Aeroflot, and then for the same reasons as the GRU in consular affairs. The merchant navy is almost identical, the only difference being that the officers there are selected to study cruisers and submarines and not strategic aviation. An organisation of exceptional importance to both services is the Trade Representation, that is the organ of the Ministry of External Trade. Literally swarming with KGB and GRU officers, this organisation provides exceptional access to business people whom both strive to exploit for their own ends. Representation in Tass, APN, *Pravda* and *Izvestia* are almost forbidden ground for the GRU. Even the KGB in this field has very narrow powers. Press matters are very carefully kept in the Central Committee's own hands, therefore KGB officers and officers of the GRU do not occupy key posts in these organisations. This does not mean of course that their secret activities suffer in any way.

Intourist is in the KGB's hands, so much so that it is not just an organisation strongly influenced by the KGB, but an actual branch of the KGB. Beginning with the construction of hotels and the putting of advertisements in the papers, and ending with the recruitment of foreigners in those same hotels, it is all run entirely by the KGB. GRU officers *are* found in Intourist, but rarely. There does exist, however, one rule which admits of no exceptions. Anything to do with the military attachés is staffed exclusively by officers of the GRU. Here there are no genuine diplomats, nor KGB. The naval, military and air attachés are regarded by the GRU as its particular brand of cover. In the West one is accustomed to see in these people not spies but military diplomats, and one assumes that this has spread to one's Soviet colleagues. This deep misapprehension is fully exploited by the GRU. Whenever you talk to a Soviet military attaché, remember always that before you stands at the very least an operational officer of an undercover residency who is faced with the problem of recruiting foreigners and who, if he does not recruit a single foreigner, sees all his other work become insignificant and all his hopes of a shining career crash to the ground. Look into his eyes and ask him how much longer he has to serve in this hospitable country and if in his answer you perceive a note of anguish, then be on your guard, for he will recruit you if he can. But perhaps he is happy with life and his eyes express pleasure. This means he has recruited one of your fellow-countrymen. Possibly there even stands in front of you a deputy resident or the GRU resident himself. Fear him and be careful of him. He is dangerous. He is experienced and cunning like an old hand should be. This is not his first time abroad, and that means he has already chalked up a significant number of successful recruits.

*

Every GRU officer in an undercover residency, whatever his official duties may be, and under whatever cover he masquerades, has his place in the general structure of the secret hierarchy. What we see in daily life is only the performance the GRU wishes to show us. Internal relations in an undercover residency have no bearing whatsoever on external, official ranks. Military ranks play an insignificant role. The important role is the actual job of the officer in the residency. There have been cases where residents with an eye to cover have occupied completely insignificant posts within embassies. At the same time the resident remains the resident and his authority is unshakeable. Within the residency he remains the strict, tyrannical, frequently wilful boss who during his briefings will frequently attack the military attachés – even though in his life as seen by the outside world he plays the part of doorman for those same attachés. The second most important person, the deputy resident, may only be a lieutenant-colonel with operational officers who are colonels but this does not prevent him from talking to them as he would to captains or lieutenants. They are only operational officers, while the GRU has decreed that he, a lieutenant-colonel, is better than them, full colonels though they may be, and has given him full powers to dispose of them and order them about. Official cover again plays absolutely no part. An operational officer may assume the official duty of assistant to a military attaché or military attaché himself, but still have the deputy resident as his own personal driver. The deputy resident is no way suffers from this. His situation is analogous to that of the Sicilian waiter who, off duty, is senior in rank to the restaurant owner within the Mafia hierarchy.

All operational officers are legal equals, from senior lieutenants to full colonels. Their seniority in the residency, however, is established by the resident exclusively on the basis of the quantity and quality of their recruitments. Recruitment work is the sole criterion for all GRU officers, regardless of age, rank or official duties. Their relations with each other in the residency might be compared with the relationships existing between fighter pilots in time of war. They also, in their own circle, pay little attention to length of service or military rank. Their criterion of respect for a man is the number of enemy aircraft he has shot down, and a lieutenant who has shot down ten aircraft may patronisingly slap on the shoulder a major who has not shot down a single aircraft. The attitude of the operational staff engaged in recruitment work to other officers may be summed up by comparison with the attitude of the fliers and the ground staff at a fighter base: 'I fly in the sky and you shovel shit.' The only exception to this attitude is the radio/cipher officer, to whom all show the greatest respect, because he knows much more about intelligence matters concerning the residency than the deputy resident.

*

Let us take a typically large residency as an example and examine it. Everything is factual. The resident is a Major-General A and his official cover (relatively unimportant), is First Secretary, Embassy. Directly beneath him are a group of five radio/cipher officers, three very experienced operational officers (one of whom runs an agent group, and two others who run especially valuable agent-sources), and four deputy residents. They are:

Colonel B, cover Deputy Trade Representative. He has twelve GRU officers below him, all working in the Trade Representation. He is in contact with one agent. One of his officers runs an agent group of three agents. Another is in contact with two agents and a third officer has one agent. The remaining officers have as yet no agents.

Lt-Colonel C, cover Assistant to the Naval Attaché. He has many operational officers beneath him, two of whom work in the Merchant Navy Representation, three in Aeroflot, five in the Embassy and ten in the departments of the Military, Naval and Air Attachés. All three of the military departments are considered to be a diplomatic unit independent from each other and from the Embassy. However, in this case, all officers entering the three military departments including the three attachés are beneath one assistant military attaché. The deputy resident is in contact with one agent. Twelve other operational officers subordinate to him have one agent each. The remainder have acquaintances who are to be recruited within one to two years. In addition to his agent-running work, this deputy resident is responsible for information work in the whole residency.

Colonel D, cover First Secretary, Embassy (deputy resident for illegals). This deputy resident has no agent and does not carry out recruitment work. He has no officers beneath him, but when he is carrying out operations in the interests of illegals, he can make use of any of the best officers of the first and second groups.

Lt-Colonel E, cover Second Secretary, Embassy. He is in contact with one agent. One operational officer is subordinate to him, disguised as the military attaché's driver, and this officer runs an agent group. In addition, this deputy resident controls the following: one technical service group (six officers), one group for the study of operational conditions (four officers), one group of operational technique (two officers), the radio monitoring station (three officers), five officers of the internal security guards for the residency and one accounts officer.

*

In all there are sixty-seven officers in the residency, of whom forty-one are operational staff, twenty operational technological staff and six technical staff. The residency has thirty-six agents, of whom twenty-five work independently of each other.

In some cases part of the undercover residency, under the command of one of the deputy residents, functions in another city permanently detached from the basic forces of the main residency. This is true, for example, of Holland, where the undercover residency is located in The Hague but part of the residency is in Amsterdam. Such an arrangement complicates work to a considerable degree but in the opinion of the GRU it is better to have two small residencies than one big one. In this case any failure in one of the residencies does not reflect on the activities of the other. Everywhere it is possible, the GRU endeavours to organise new, independent residencies. For this it has to observe two basic conditions: the presence of official Soviet diplomatic representation – an embassy, consulate, military attaché's department, military communications mission or a permanent UN mission; and the presence of an officially registered radio station in direct contact with Moscow. Where these two conditions obtain, residencies can be quickly organised, even the very smallest possible, consisting of two men but independent and self-contained.

Apart from the security angle, this practice also ensures parallelism, as the GRU can control one resident by means of another. Such possibilities are open to Soviet intelligence in many countries. For example, in Paris there is one of the most expansionist undercover residencies of the GRU. Independent of it in Marseilles there is another, smaller residency. Their performance is vastly enhanced by the fierce competition between them. In West Germany the GRU has been able to create five residencies. Wherever there is official Soviet diplomatic representation with radio transmission, there is also an undercover residency of the GRU. In many cases there is also an undercover residency of the KGB. But while the residencies of the GRU are organised in any official mission – civil, military or mixed – those of the KGB are not. In Marseilles, New York, Amsterdam, Geneva and Montreal the Soviet missions are clearly civil, and in all these cities there are undercover residencies of both KGB and GRU. But where the mission is clearly military, as for example the Soviet observation mission in West Germany, the KGB may not have a residency. This also applies to the numerous missions of Soviet military advisers in developing countries. The KGB presence there is only for the maintenance of security among the genuine military advisers.

In speaking about the undercover residency we must not forget to mention another category of people participating in espionage activities – co-opted personnel. These are Soviet citizens abroad who are not officers of the GRU or the KGB, but fulfil a number of tasks set them by these organisations. The co-opted person may be of any rank from doorman to ambassador and he carries out very different tasks, from studies of the foreigners surrounding him to clearing dead-letter boxes. The KGB has always been interested in the exploitation of co-opted persons; following the principle of 'don't stick your own neck out if you can get somebody else to stick it out for you'. The GRU is not so keen, using co-opted persons only in exceptional cases. Its guiding principle is: 'don't trust even your best friend with your motor car, girlfriend – or agent'. The rewards for a co-opted person are monetary ones which, unlike the basic salary, are not subject to tax. Usually in every embassy, consulate and trade representation, out of every ten 'clean' officials, seven are co-opted onto the KGB staff, one onto the GRU staff; only the remaining two are clean. Either they are complete idiots, or the sons of members of the Central Committee whom wild horses could not force to have anything to do with intelligence. In other words, in Soviet official institutions, it is a very, very tricky matter indeed to meet a man who has no connections with intelligence.

Chapter Three

Agents

In present-day Soviet intelligence terminology the term 'agent' has only one meaning. An agent is a foreigner recruited by Soviet intelligence and carrying out secret tasks on its behalf. All agents, irrespective of the group or section of the GRU to which they belong, are divided into two groups: the basic agent and the supplementary agent. Basic agents fall into four categories: they are residents or group leaders; they are providers of information; they are executive agents whose main task is to kill; or they are recruiting agents. In the supplementary group are wireless operators, legalising agents, documentalists, the owners of safe houses, addresses, telephones and radio transmission points.

Head Agents
Head agents are the leaders of agent groups and agent residents. Head agents are selected from the most experienced agents available, men and women who have had long years of service and have given proof of their devotion to duty. They are invested with wide powers and possess significant financial independence. In cases where the organisation entrusted to them collapses, the head agent must take the decision to do away with unwanted people who pose a threat to it. In this and other emergencies he can always count on the full support of the GRU.

The difference between the group leader and the agent resident is that the group leader may take a whole range of important decisions concerning the group entrusted to him, but he may not recruit agents at all. The agent resident has a wider range of interests, the most important being recruitment. The group leader may be subordinate to the residency, to the illegal, undercover or agent residency or directly to the Centre, but the agent resident may only be subordinate to the Centre.

Sources

These are agents who directly obtain secret information, documents or samples of military technology and weaponry. In the recruitment of such people, it is first and foremost their access to political, military, technological and other secrets which is taken into account. It is clearly unnecessary to recruit an officer from the Ministry of Defence if one can recruit his secretary. In other words, the GRU has contact with people occupying relatively unimportant posts but with possibly greater knowledge than their superiors. With this in mind, apart from secretaries, the people of special interest to the GRU are workers in printing and typing offices which produce secret documents, cipher officers, diplomatic couriers, computer operators, communications clerks, draughtsmen and other technical personnel.

Executive Agents

These are agents recruited to carry out assassinations, diversions or sabotage. The recruitment of executive agents is not usually carried out by the central GRU, but by the local organs of the GRU—the military district departments. Sometimes even strategic intelligence needs similar specialists, but in smaller number.

Executive agents are recruited from criminal elements and from that band of naturally brutish characters who, with passing time, become accustomed to executing any orders they are given. Frequently agents who have been acting as providers of information are transferred by both the strategic and operational branches of the GRU to the category of executive agent, in cases where they may have lost their access.

Agent Recruiters

These are the most devoted and thoroughly tested agents, people who either never had access or who have lost it. As their name suggests, the GRU uses them solely for the recruitment of new agents. The most successful will eventually become group leader or sometimes agent resident.

Agent Legalisers

These are subsidiary agents. They work in the interests of illegals and as a rule are recruited and run only by illegals. Candidates for this category of agents are sought among officials of the police and passport departments, consular clerks, customs and immigration officials, and small employers of labour. Agent legalisers are subjected to especially thorough vetting, because the fate of illegals is entrusted to them. When a Soviet illegal arrives in a country the task of the legalising agent is to ensure the issue of documents by making the necessary entries in the registration books and to ensure that the illegal is in possession of the necessary documentation.

In the history of the GRU quite a few priests carrying falsified documents and registers of baptism and death have given immense service to illegals who, on the basis of false entries, have been able to obtain the necessary documents. A similar role to that of the legalising agent is played by the *documentation agents*. These are recruited by the undercover residency and their job is to obtain passports, driving licences and samples of official police forms. In contradistinction to the legalising agents, documentation agents do not have any direct contact with illegals. Although they obtain tens and sometimes hundreds, even thousands of passports, they have no direct knowledge of how and when the GRU is going to use them. Frequently the GRU uses the passports obtained through the good offices of documentation agents only as a sample for the preparation of similar falsified copies. Documentation agents may be recruited from among criminal classes who are occupied with the forging and selling of documents on the black market and also from clerks concerned with the production, inventory, storage and issue of passports. Frequently documentation agents have successfully worked among poor students, persuading them, for a financial consideration, to lose their passports.

Couriers

These are supplementary agents engaged in transporting agent materials over state frontiers. Obviously it is not necessary to employ special couriers to transport the material into the Soviet Union or its satellites.

The basic flow of agent material which is not subject to particular suspicion goes from countries with hard regimes into countries with more soft regimes. In the opinion of the GRU, an opinion fortified by the experience of many years, the hardest country is Great Britain, followed by France, the United States, the Federal Republic of Germany, Belgium and Holland. As soft countries the GRU includes Finland, Ireland and Austria among others.

The GRU also makes very wide use of countries of the Third World for this purpose, and couriers may sometimes make very long journeys before the material finally arrives in the hands of the GRU. Examples are known of material obtained in the United States going first to Latin America, then to Africa and only from Africa being conveyed to the Soviet Union. In recruiting couriers, the GRU pays particular attention to the drivers and guards of long-distance trains, commercial travellers and sailors of merchant fleets. When hi-jacking of aircraft became more frequent and controls at airports became stricter, the GRU virtually gave up recruiting the crews of airliners. If it uses these at all, it is only for transporting small-sized non-metallic objects.

The Owner of a Safe House or Flat

He is a supplementary agent occupying a position of great trust, usually recruited from among house-owners, concierges and hotel owners, in a word, all those who possess not one but several flats or dwelling places. The term 'safe flat' should be understood not only in its generally accepted meaning but also as a well-equipped cellar, attic, garage or store. For safe flats the GRU selects quiet secluded places where they may want to be able to hide a man sometimes for a length of several months; to carry out meetings, briefings and de-briefings; to change clothes and change appearances; and to hide stolen materials and photograph stolen documents. The owner of a safe house or flat is known in the colloquial language of the GRU by the abbreviation 'KK'.

The Safe Address Owner

He is an agent who receives and transmits secret messages for the GRU, usually recruited from among those people who receive copious correspondence from abroad; the work is normally restricted to inhabitants of 'soft' countries. Sources who have obtained information and intelligence in hard countries send letters in SW to these addresses and the owners transmit the correspondence to officers of the undercover residency. One interesting aspect of recruitment is that the GRU prefers middle-aged people who would not be affected by general mobilisation in the country, so that the chain of communication is not interrupted.

The possessors of secret telephones and, more recently, tele-printers are recruited by the same rules applied to the owners of secret addresses. In GRU language these types of agent networks and their possessors are known by the abbreviations 'KA', 'KT', 'KTP'.

The owners of transmitting points are used for transmitting agent materials within the limits of one city or area. Usually they are street sellers in small kiosks, stalls or paper stalls. An agent who has acquired intelligence will stop and hand over the material to the owner. Hours later, sometimes days, GRU officers will visit the stall to collect the material and hand over money for the agents together with new instructions. This avoids direct contact between the GRU and the agent. Increased security might mean the source agent using a dead-letter box which the stall holder will empty, not knowing who has filled it. The GRU will announce the dead-letter box's whereabouts to the transmitting point only after it has been filled. A different one will be used for each operation, and so even if the police discover that the GRU has a special interest in the small shop or stall and subsequently establishes that this stall serves as a transmitting point, it will still be very difficult to discover the source agent. To mount a surveillance operation in the neighbourhood of the dead-letter box is impossible since the transmitting point only acquires its location after it has been filled; the agent himself has disappeared long before. The transmitting point is known by the abbreviation 'PP'.

*

In examining different kinds of agents, people from the free world who have sold themselves to the GRU, one cannot avoid touching on yet another category, perhaps the least appealing of all. Officially one is not allowed to call them agents, and they are not agents in the full sense of being recruited agents. We are talking about the numerous members of overseas societies of friendship with the Soviet Union. Officially, all Soviet representatives regard these parasites with touching feelings of friendship, but privately they call them 'shit-eaters' ('*govnoed*'). It is difficult to say where this expression originated, but it is truly the only name they deserve. The use of this word has become so firmly entrenched in Soviet embassies that it is impossible to imagine any other name for these people. A conversation might run as follows: 'Today we've got a friendship evening with shit-eaters', or 'Today we're having some shit-eaters to dinner. Prepare a suitable menu'.

Officers of both the GRU and the KGB have very much more respect for their agents than for the shit-eaters. The motives of agents are clear – an easy life and plenty of money. If you take risks and lose, then no money and no easy life. To the end of his life the agent will not be able to tear himself away from this servitude – as is the case in the criminal world. But the behaviour of the numerous friends of the Soviet Union is utterly incomprehensible to Soviet people. In the Soviet Union everybody without exception wishes to be abroad, to go absolutely anywhere, even if only with one eye to look at Mongolia or Cambodia. Oh! to be abroad, is the cry, led by the children of Brezhnev, Gromyko and Andropov. When Soviet people want to say that a thing is outstandingly good, they say, 'Really, this must be foreign.' It does not matter which country it comes from, or what its quality or age – it has to be foreign. But suddenly one finds these friends of the Soviet Union, who enjoy all the fruits of civilisation down to Gillette razor blades, who can buy anything they want in the shops, even bananas, and yet they praise the Soviet Union. No, these people are nothing but shit-eaters according to Soviet Intelligence. The contempt felt for them does not prevent the GRU and KGB from using them whenever they can. They do everything free, and they will even come to meetings in secure places like the Soviet Embassy.

The recruitment of such people is not recommended by the Central Committee, but why bother to recruit them when they bring such advantages without being recruited? The GRU usually makes use of the shit-eaters 'in the dark', in other words not saying what they are used for or how much they benefit from their services. They usually ask from them information about their neighbours, friends, acquaintances, fellow workers and so on. Sometimes one of them is asked to organise an evening party with one or another of his acquaintances, after which the GRU thanks him and tells him to forget what has happened. They are very good people, they forget everything.

Chapter Four

Agent Recruiting

Agent recruiting is the most important task of both strategic and operational intelligence. No real problems can be solved without agent penetration in basic government, military and technological centres of the enemy.

In the previous chapter we examined the types of secret agents and also the various differences between them. It would not be an exaggeration to say that any citizen of the West, having been recruited by the GRU, may be used very effectively for intelligence purposes, some for the acquisition of secret documents, some for assassinating people, and some for the transporting of agent materials. No citizen of any age and either sex would be idle for long once he or she fell into the hands of the GRU. Nevertheless, basic importance is attached to the provider of information. Long experience has persuaded the GRU that it is essential above all to recruit sources, and only after the GRU has acquired through these sources all possible material may the source himself be used for other purposes, as a recruiter, head agent or supplementary agent. The GRU is convinced that a former source who is now working, for example, as the owner of a transmitting point will never on his own initiative go to the police; but the same cannot be said of agents who have never provided secrets for the GRU, who have not had firm contacts with them. The search for suitable candidates is implemented at the same time in certain different ways: the scrupulous collection of information on persons of interest to the GRU including government institutions for staffs, military bases, design bureaux and people connected with these targets; the study of all foreigners without exception who have any contacts at all with officers of the GRU; and the gradual widening of circles of acquaintances among foreigners. If an operational officer has a hundred acquaintances, one of these must surely be a potential provider of information which will be of interest.

A candidate for recruitment must fulfil the following conditions: he must have agent potential, that is he must be in the position to provide information of real use to the GRU, either to steal or copy secrets, to communicate secret information by word of mouth, or to recruit new agents. There must exist motives by means of which he may be recruited – displeasure with the regime or other political motives, personal financial problems, or private motives like a desire for revenge on somebody or secret crimes which he is trying to hide. It is desirable that he be sympathetic to communism without being a communist. Communist parties everywhere have been compromised to a certain extent by their contacts with the KGB and the GRU, and it is always recommended that agents recruited from communist parties should leave the party.

After the selection of a candidate for recruitment, the second stage – tracing and vetting – commences. Details are collected about the candidate, details which may be obtained through reference books, telephone directories and the press; the task of obtaining all available information about the candidate may well be given to other agents. The GRU may equally want a surveillance on him to collect extra data about his daily life. This process sometimes gives very gratifying results. Up to now the person himself does not suspect that the GRU exists and he has had no contact with its representatives, but it already has a considerable wealth of detail on him. Subsequently the GRU enters the process of cultivation, which consists in a further definition of motives which will be used in the actual recruitment of the person. It also tries to exacerbate his weaknesses: for example, if the man experiences financial problems, the GRU will endeavour to make them worse. If he is displeased with the political regime, the GRU will endeavour to turn his displeasure into hatred. The cultivation process may be carried out after the establishment of an acquaintanceship with the candidate. The whole process, from the beginning of the search for a candidate to the completion of a cultivation period, normally extends for not less than a year; only after this does actual recruitment take place.

There are two principal methods of recruitment, the gradual approach and the crash approach. The crash approach is the highest class of agent work. The GRU may authorise the resident to mount such an operation only if the resident has been able to provide good arguments for the taking of such a risk. Quite a few examples are known of recruitment at the first meeting, of course following the secret cultivation which has gone on for many months. It was in this way that many American creators of the first atomic bomb were recruited. Their subsequent argument was that it was as a mark of protest against the bombing of the Japanese cities that they, on their own initiative, established contact with Soviet intelligence. However, for some reason they forgot to add that this contact had been established long before the first experiments with the bomb, when there was no cause for protest. They also evaded the question as to how several people, simultaneously and independently from one another, established contact with the undercover residency of the GRU in Canada, but not with the undercover residency of the KGB in Mexico, for example.

The crash approach, or 'love at first sight' in GRU jargon, has a number of irrefutable advantages. Contact with the future agent takes place only once, instead of at meetings over many months, as is the case with the gradual approach. After the first contact the newly recruited agent will himself take action on his own security. He will never talk to his wife, or tell her that he has a charming friend in the Soviet military attaché who is also very interested in stamp collecting.

In the gradual approach method, this sort of thing happens very, very often. The candidate has as yet not felt the deadly grip of the GRU, has not yet understood what it wants from him. He still nourishes his illusions, and naturally he will not hide his good friendship with such charming people. However, the gradual approach method, despite its shortcomings, is frequently used. The fact is that the GRU is not always, indeed not even in the majority of cases, able to collect a sufficient amount of material about the candidate without his knowledge to prepare him sufficiently for recruitment. In many cases it is necessary to establish contact and to use each meeting with the candidate to study his motives and to carry out vetting and cultivation.

Having established contact, the operational officer tries by every possible method to avoid 'blowing' the candidate; that is, he tries to hide the connection from the police, from friends and acquaintances of the man himself, and also from his own fellow countrymen. The only people who should know anything about an agent and therefore about candidates for recruitment are the resident, the deputy resident and of course the cipher officer and the Centre – nobody else. In order that he should not blow the candidate from the very first meeting, the operational officer will try to carry out meetings in secluded restaurants, cafés, bars far from the place where the candidate lives and far from his place of work. At all costs he will try to avoid the candidate telephoning him either at home or in the embassy. He will try to avoid the candidate visiting Soviet official institutions and places where Soviet people gather together. He will decline invitations to meet the candidate's family or visit his home. (The particular pretexts I used were that my office was far too busy, or I was never there, so the candidate would not ring; at home, I would tell him, there was a small baby who slept badly. Of course, in order to appear serious, I had to give him the telephone numbers with my business card.) After the acquaintanceship has ripened, the GRU officer will try to make every subsequent meeting as interesting and useful as possible for the candidate. If they exchange postage stamps, then the Soviet, by apparent mistake or out of friendship, will give the future agent a very valuable stamp. The officer may then ask for a very innocent and insignificant favour from the man and pay him very generously for it. During this stage the most important thing is that the future agent becomes accustomed to being asked favours and fulfilling them accurately. It does not matter what sort of favours or services. Maybe he will be asked to accept at his address and forward to the officers letters ostensibly from his mistress, or to buy a complete set of telephone directories and give them to the officer as if he did not know how or where this could be done. By degrees the tasks become more complicated, but the payment for them grows equally. Perhaps he will be asked to acquire in his name some works of reference which are not on sale and are distributed only on signature, or he will be asked to talk about and describe his friends who work with him. In many cases the actual recruitment proposal is never made, as the candidate gradually becomes an agent of the GRU without having fully realised it. He may consider that he is simply doing his business and doing favours for a good friend. Then, much to his surprise, the man will one day find that all ways of extricating himself have been cut off, and that he is deeply ensnared in espionage work. After he has become aware of this for himself, the GRU informs him what the affair is all about and there begins a new stage. The tasks become more serious but the payment for them gradually decreases. This is done on the pretext of his own security. What can he do? Go on strike?

There exists yet another method of recruitment, perhaps the most effective and secure. This method was worked out by the GRU in the first decade after the war and seems not to be used by the KGB. It can only be used at exhibitions and only against the owners of small firms which produce military material. In spite of the fact that the method has so many limitations, including the impossibility of recruiting generals and their secretaries, and equally its complete unacceptability for illegals it does, however, give positive results. It is very similar to the direct approach, but is distinct from the classical 'love at first sight' in that a lengthy search for a candidate, his tracing, vetting and cultivation are absent.

Before the opening of exhibitions of military electronics, armaments and military technology, ship-building and engine-building conferences, air shows and so on, hundreds of which take place every year, a scientific delegation appears at the GRU residency with a list of everything which is essential for the Soviet military and the armaments industry. The experts of course know that at the exhibition there will be demonstrations of models whose sale to the Soviet Union is categorically prohibited. None the less, the delegation will carry suitcases crammed full of money, with full powers to spend it as they wish. All expenditure is approved and justified. The examination and construction of such samples as they have been able to obtain in the Soviet Union will occupy much more time and money. The delegation visits the exhibition and looks at the stands of the big corporations only to disguise its real object. At each of these stands these are several salesmen and guides, any one or all of which may be from the security services. The delegation is only really interested in the stands of small firms where the explanations are carried out by the owner or a director himself. The delegation gets into conversation with him and an officer of the local GRU residency acts the part of interpreter. The experts pass themselves off as an official Soviet delegation. At the same time they manage to let the operational

110

officer know that they have arrived at just such a firm as could be of use to them and that the exhibit is not just a model, but an actual piece. 'Is it really forbidden to buy such a piece? Oh! What a pity. Nothing to be done, but tell us, how much does it cost? 20,000? How cheap! We would pay twenty times that much for such a piece! Great pity that it is not for sale.' All this in a light-hearted way, as if incidental. The conversation turns to another subject. After a few minutes the delegation takes its leave in a friendly way. The interpreter stays behind for a few seconds. 'It was so nice meeting you. Could we not continue our talk over dinner this evening? No? You're busy? What a pity. Many thanks. It was very nice to make your acquaintance.' And that is all, nothing criminal, just a short, friendly conversation. The Soviet delegation did not propose anything to anybody. It did not ask, it did not demand. It was merely interested. In the meantime the delegation goes on with its inspection. The exhibition is huge, hundreds of firms, and the list of essential things is too long. Another stand, another firm, the same result, it does not matter. Not everything has been lost. There are still more stands. 'How much does this piece cost? 25,000? Only 25,000, we would give half a million for that. Great pity that it's not for sale.' The delegation goes on. The interpreter stays for a few seconds. 'Could I not invite you to dinner this evening in the restaurant?' 'I don't know whether that would be all right. We hardly know each other.' And that is all. Recruitment is accomplished. The delegation continues its inspection. New interpreters are provided. Drinking martinis in the bar, they wait their turn. The exhibition is huge. Hundreds of firms and the list of equipment wanted by their government is very long.

The GRU's calculation has shown itself to be unfailing. The owner of a small firm, even a very successful one, is always at great risk, always keen to strengthen his situation. When he receives a proposal to sell his own wares at a price fifteen to twenty times the highest normal price, he thinks to himself: this is a matter of industrial espionage, which in several countries is not even considered a criminal offence. From the first moment he knows what is wanted from him and carefully evaluates the step that he decides on. In any case, if he sells his product he can hide the fact from the authorities. It is equally easy for him to hide the money he has received. The only thing he has not taken into consideration is the wolf-like greed of the GRU. He hopes to dispose of the products of his firm, supposing that this will be sufficient. He is deeply mistaken. Having bought the first model or set of documents, certainly at a staggering price, the GRU will later on lower the prices and finally dictate them. One might object that the really big secrets are all in the hands of the big firms, but this is not absolutely true. Very often Soviet designers are not interested in the whole rocket or the whole aircraft, but only in some small part – an engine, a steering system or some particular instrument (in many cases not even an important part but only a membrane, a heat sink or some such thing) – exactly the sort of thing that would be produced by a components manufacturer. And of course recruitment in small firms does not in any way hinder the GRU's attempts to penetrate large firms. Far from it. After he has been milked, the owner of a components manufacturing firm, now turned agent, must turn his attention to the recruitment of other agents in the big firms to which he supplies his parts. Then suddenly in the Soviet Union an aircraft exactly like Concorde appears. (To blame the GRU for the trials and difficulties of the TU144 Concordski is not justified. Weak Soviet industry, using antediluvian technology, was simply not able to copy the aeroplane properly, despite having all the necessary drawings and documents.) Recently, the number of exhibition recruitments by the GRU has steadily increased. They have been facilitated by the fact that in these recruitments the GRU does not spend one rouble of its own money. The money which the delegation brings with it to the exhibition comes out of the budget of the armaments industry which is ready to spend as much money as it has to in profitable business. For its money the armaments industry receives essential documents and samples, and the GRU, without paying a penny, receives an agent who will serve it for long years afterwards. Exhibition recruitments are also attractive because they can be carried out with complete impunity. Only one case of detection is known, an air show at Le Bourget when the assistant Soviet military attaché was detained for endeavouring to carry out just such a recruitment. He was detained, but not for long because a military diplomat cannot be held. Declared *persona non grata*, after three years he went to another country in another official capacity as a deputy resident. The only thing which is not clear in all these stories is the attitude of those countries who joyfully accept these supposed 'diplomats'.

As for GRU illegals, they basically use the first two methods. The work of illegals of course is made easier by the obvious simplification of the search for candidates and their tracing and vetting. Since they very often play the part of *bona fide* business people they come into frequent contact with the owners of firms producing military material, and by means of proposing advantageous deals, they gradually attract these people to play the part of agents. There is another very important factor. Illegals hardly ever recruit in the name of Soviet intelligence. They always assume another guise. In Japan, for example, they may pass themselves off as American industrial spies, in Northern Ireland as an organisation going in for terrorist activities against the English military presence, in Arab countries as anti-Zionists. In countries with dictatorial regimes GRU illegals recruit people in the name of anti-government organisations carrying on the underground struggle against tyranny. A method often used by illegals is to pass themselves off as supporters of separatist movements. It is only necessary for the illegal to know some of the important political views in order to be able to adopt them for himself and begin recruiting. Sometimes such recruitments are implemented very quickly and without problems. 'We are representatives of such and such a liberation army, this or that red brigade. Can't you help us? If you can't we ask you not to let anybody know about our visit.' The candidate is then recruited in the name of an organisation for which he feels sympathy and he gratifies his conscience all his life with the thought that he is a revolutionary and defends ideals near to his heart, not even suspecting the existence of the GRU and its illegals. He is so full of pride that he has been selected for such secret work that he may not even tell those who think likewise about it.

There is one last method of recruiting. This is when a foreigner comes in and says, 'Please recruit me.' However strange it may seem, every year hundreds of such people come into Soviet embassies and the same answer awaits them all. 'This is a diplomatic representation and not an espionage centre. Be so kind as to leave the building or we will call the police.' The police are usually not called but the embassy staff chase the would-be agent out quickly. Even if the GRU (and the KGB, for that matter) is sure that the caller is not a young reporter anxious to publish a sensational article or somebody purporting to sell secret documents but really only selling some nonsense, how can they be sure that the caller is not a police agent who wants to know who in the embassy is concerned with secrets? Thus the answer to all is the same. 'You have got the wrong address. We are not concerned with such things.' This does not mean that it would not be interesting to have a look at what the caller has brought, but long experience has shown that the person who really wants to be recruited and really has something to sell does not say very much but simply hands over the material, together with instructions as to where he can be found, and leaves. He might add a note to the effect that 'this is not all the material I have but only a part, if you are interested.'

Elementary psychological analysis shows that this is perhaps the only way to convince the GRU that they can trust the person. Indeed if a person has decided to entrust his life and the happiness of his family to such dark and unknown personalities, why on earth should he not hand them some papers? By such a gesture he not only draws attention to himself but he gives time for reflection on his proposals and for the necessary checking with higher authorities and checking of the material. However, if the visitor brings papers and documents to the embassy and begins to demand immediate financial reward, this leads one to think, 'If, after careful consideration, he has decided on this step, if he is really ready to entrust his life to us, why does he think that we would deceive him and not return the papers if they were of no use to us? And where is the guarantee that the papers which he has brought are not forgeries? Who would carry the can if we paid him money for papers which afterwards turned out to be forgeries? No, we are not interested in such things.'

That these 'walk-ins' are an extremely unpredictable form of recruitment is perhaps best illustrated by two examples, both of which occurred at the same residency in West Germany. An American sergeant came to one of the Soviet observation missions in West Germany (each of which is a GRU residency), bringing with him the block of a cipher machine used in one of the American bases. The sergeant announced that for a certain sum he could bring a second part of the machine and added that there could only be a deal on condition that the GRU would not subsequently attempt to recruit him. The residency immediately accepted both proposals. The sergeant got his money and an assurance that the GRU would forget all about him immediately after the deal was done.

The cipher machine which was obtained, or more accurately two of its basic blocks, enabled the technical services of the GRU to decipher thousands of American radio communications which had been intercepted earlier but remained undeciphered. They also enabled them to study the principles of cipher work in the American Army and in the armies of its allies and, by exploiting the American principles, to create more complete Soviet examples. What about the sergeant? Of course he was immediately recruited. . . .

On another occasion a couple of years later an American major approached the same Soviet residency proposing to sell an American atomic artillery shell. In proof of his good intentions he handed over free of charge to the residency detailed plans of the atomic depots and instructions on checking procedures and standing orders for work with atomic equipment. These documents by themselves were of great value, although the major's main proposal was of vastly greater interest. The major announced that he would demand a substantial sum for the shell, and imposed the condition that the Soviet side, having studied the shell, must return it after two months. Some days later, the specialists of the GRU information service confirmed the genuineness and very great importance of the documents which had been acquired. The GRU leadership decided to buy the atomic shell and to pay the price demanded for it by the American. A number of the senior officers of the residency were called to Moscow and given a crash course in American atomic technology. A week later, on a dark rainy night in a clearing in the middle of a forest, two motor cars met. In one was the American major, in the other three operational officers. There were two more Soviet cars hidden nearby, ready to intervene if necessary. Many people did without sleep that night. The Soviet Consul dozed by his telephone, in full readiness to come tearing out to the wood and in the name of the Union of Soviet Socialist Republics to defend the military diplomats. On the orders of the Central Committee, many highly placed officials in the Ministry of Foreign Affairs and Tass were also on alert. Of course they did not know what was going on or where, but they were ready to announce to the world that the imperialists had mounted yet another provocation against the

Soviet Union. In fact, the Tass and Ministry of Foreign Affairs announcements were already prepared. But everything went according to plan. The American and the three Soviets transferred the shell from one car to the other, and a thorough check was carried out. The operational officers knew beforehand the serial number, the level of radiation, the exact weight and the markings which would identify it as a genuine shell. All was as it should be. The Soviets handed over a briefcase full of banknotes to the American and agreed to meet in two months' time for the return of the shell. Once the shell was in the Soviet car with diplomatic number plates, it was tantamount to being on Soviet territory. The police could stop the car, but they did not have the right to search it nor remove anything from it. Diplomatic immunity is not to be trifled with. In the event nobody stopped the officers, and the car drove peacefully into the courtyard of the Soviet diplomatic mission. Later the shell was transported in a diplomatic container under armed guard to the Soviet Union.

The GRU chief joyfully informed the Central Committee of the successful outcome of the operation. 'Where is the bomb?' asked a voice on the telephone. 'We have it in GRU headquarters.' 'In Moscow!?' 'Yes.'

A long and largely unprintable tirade ensued, whose import was roughly as follows: 'And what happens if there is a little spring inside this shell and it explodes right in the middle of the Soviet capital and turns Moscow into Hiroshima?'

The GRU had worked out the whole operation with the maximum number of precautionary measures and the plan to acquire the shell had been confirmed by all departments from the chief to the general staff up to the Central Committee. However, nobody had foreseen the possibility that there could be a timed device in the shell and that the Central Committee, the Politburo, the KGB, the GRU, all the Ministers and departments of State, the general staff, all the Military Academies, all the principal design bureaux, in a word, everything which constitutes Soviet power, could be instantaneously destroyed. There was no answer. No defence was possible. One shell and the whole system could have gone up, because everybody and everything is controlled from Moscow. The possibility of such an occurrence had only been realised in the Central Committee when the shell was already in Moscow. Instead of the expected decoration, the GRU chief received a 'service incompetence note' – a strong warning that in the future even the most trivial mistake would lead to dismissal.

The shell was taken for the time being to the central aerodrome and a military transport aircraft speedily transported it to Novaya Zemlya. The shell did not explode. At the same time there was no guarantee that it would not explode while it was being dismantled and destroy the leading Soviet specialists who were working on it, so the dismantling was conducted in a special pavilion hurriedly constructed on the atomic testing ground. Preliminary work on the shell had already disquieted the Soviet specialists, as it was much more radioactive than it should have been. After protracted arguments and consultations, the shell was dismantled with the greatest possible care. Only then was it found that it was not a shell at all – but a beautifully executed copy.

The American major from the depot for atomic armaments had known to the last detail how to do this. He had taken a written-off practice shell or, as it is called, a 'standard weight equivalent', had painted it as a real shell and put on a corresponding marking and number. Inside the shell he had put some radioactive waste which he had obtained. Of course he was not able to regulate this to the extent that the level of radiation would conform to the level of radiation of a genuine shell, but this was not necessary. At the time when it was first checked after having been handed over to the operational officers, there had been no attempt to determine the exact level of radioactivity. The officers had only been interested to see whether there was radiation or not. After all that had happened the officers who had taken part in the operation, of course, received no decorations but at the same time they were not punished and neither was the GRU chief. The Special Commission of the General Staff and Central Committee established that the forgery had been very skilfully and thoroughly executed and that there had been little possibility of exposing it at the time of the hand-over. All the same the GRU was not happy about it. It began a search for the American major. The first attempts proved unsuccessful. It was established that he had been posted to the USA immediately after the sale of the forgery, and it would not be so easy to find him there. He had apparently known of the imminence of his posting and chosen his moment perfectly. Steps were taken to find him in the United States, and at the same time the GRU asked for permission to murder him from the Central

117

Committee. However, the Central Committee turned down the request on the basis that the major was incredibly cunning and could well outwit the GRU a second time as he had outwitted them earlier. They were ordered to forget about the major and stop searching for him. Now, whenever a 'walk-in' appears at a Soviet embassy and suggests the purchase for an exorbitant price of technical documents of exceptional importance, GRU residents always remember the American major.

That it is extremely difficult to find real volunteers is a simple fact. It is much, much harder to discover a volunteer than an agent whom the GRU has spent a year and more in processing. But real volunteers, however warmly they may be welcomed, do not take into consideration another simple thing. The Soviet operational officer, having seen a great deal of the ugly face of communism, very frequently feels the utmost repulsion to those who sell themselves to it willingly. Even amongst those few who still believe in communism, the intelligence officer will make a great distinction between the agent he has recruited by using a whole arsenal of tricks and traps, and the volunteer. And when a GRU or KGB officer decides to break with his criminal organisation, something which fortunately happens quite often, the first thing he will do is try to expose the hated volunteer.

Chapter Five

Agent Communications

GRU theoreticians officially admit that agent communications —
that complex of channels for transmitting instructions and material — is the weakest link in the chain. It is the fault of communications, they say, that there are so many failures, and to some
degree they are right. Whatever the theoreticians say, however, we
in the field know that by far the greatest damage to Soviet
intelligence is caused by the defection of GRU officers. Enormous
damage was done when Igor Gusenko went over to the West. By
this one gesture the whole powerful current of technological
intelligence on the production of atomic weapons, which was
flowing like a river into the hands of Stalin and his blood-thirsty
clique, was stopped dead. And historians will remember with
gratitude the name of the GRU Colonel Oleg Penkovsky. Thanks to
his priceless information the Cuban crisis was not transformed
into a last World War. Nevertheless, it is indisputable that after
the phenomenon of willing and mass defection to the side of the
enemy, which was clearly absent in the old Russian intelligence
service of the pre-revolutionary period, agent communications is
the most vulnerable sector of Soviet intelligence.

All agent communications are divided into personal and non-
personal. Personal contact is the most vulnerable element, and
preference is always given to non-personal contact. At the same
time, in the first stages, especially during cultivation, recruitment
and vetting, personal meetings are an inescapable evil with which
one has to come to terms. Later on, as agents gain experience and
involvement in their work, personal contacts gradually give way
to non-personal ones. Many of the most experienced agents have
not had a personal meeting with their case officer for several years.
If such meetings are absolutely unavoidable, the GRU prefers that
they should take place either on its own or on neutral territory.

Routine meetings are organised between agents, however. For example an illegal will meet his agent or officers of the undercover residency their agents. The details for these meetings are worked out previously. Whoever is the senior man will give instructions to the junior as to where, when, and in what circumstances they will meet. Experienced agents are often given a programme of meetings for six months ahead, sometimes a year, and in some cases even five years or more. Routine meetings usually take place in cafés, restaurants, cinemas, night clubs or parks. Both parties try to give the impression that it is a normal meeting between ordinary people discussing important topics. Frequently they will try to give the impression that they are collectors of such items as postage stamps, postcards or coins and will have these objects spread out in front of them in the restaurant or café where they are meeting. Sometimes these meetings take place in cinemas or public conveniences. Longer meetings, especially during the vetting stage of agents, will take place in hotels and camping places, caravans, yachts or boats which either are the property of the agent or are hired by him. In all cases, and this also applies to other operations involving agents, GRU officers will try to avoid city quarters which are known to be the haunt of criminals or prostitutes, and railway and police stations, airports, guarded state military or commercial undertakings – in other words all those places where police activity may be expected to be at its highest. The alternative meeting is a carbon copy of the main meeting for which arrangements are made at the same time as the main meeting: 'If one of us should be unable to get to the meeting we will meet in the same place in a week's time'. A complicated system of alternative meetings is set out for experienced agents, and there may be up to three or four alternative meetings for each main meeting. With so many alternatives it is essential that places and times are changed.

This system of alternative meetings is introduced by GRU officers long before recruitment. A man who has as yet done nothing for the GRU, who does not even suspect its existence, is already being indoctrinated into secrecy and is already being introduced to the system of agent communications. Usually the subject is introduced in various quite innocent ways; for example, the officer says, 'I shall be very pleased to meet you again but I simply don't know whether I shall be able to be on time. The life of a diplomat contains so many unexpected happenings. If I am late, then don't wait for me more than ten minutes. In any case we will meet again in three days' time.' If you have a good friend in the Soviet embassy and he says that sort of thing to you, and at the same time has a hundred reasons why he cannot use the telephone in such a simple case, be sure that the GRU has a thick file on you and that sooner or later you will receive a proposal of recruitment and notice with astonishment that all ways out seem to be blocked.

At the other end of the spectrum there is the *emergency meeting*. This access is accorded only to the most experienced agents, and those who may communicate information of such outstanding importance that it brooks no delay at all. The agent is told how he should go about calling the officer on stipulated telephones or telegrams or signals. In the same way the agent is also given the possibility of communicating danger. For example, if he rings up on the telephone and says, 'I need John,' then the officer will come immediately. If the agent says, 'Ring John,' then they will reply that he has made a mistake. If the agent uses the second variant, then he is showing the GRU that he has been arrested by the police who are trying to get to the case officer through the agent.

Brush contacts are for handing over material, instructions, money and so on. The officer and the agent carry out only one contact, in very populous places, in the underground, on full buses, at peak hours and when the crowds come out of stadiums, for example. Brush contact must be carried out with great precision otherwise the crowd may separate those taking part. On the other hand the transmission of the material must not attract attention especially if one of the participants is under strict surveillance. The *check meeting* is carried out in the same conditions as the routine meeting. However, the most junior of those taking part must not suspect that it is not a routine meeting and that he is in fact being checked. A number of GRU officers take up position before the meeting, in places where they can easily observe what is going on (for example, on observation platforms for tourists where there are powerful binoculars and telescopes installed). The entry of the agent to the meeting place is checked from a great distance. They check his punctuality, his behaviour, they watch for anybody who follows him, they observe the presence of any suspicious movement in the area of the meeting place prior to the meeting. After the agent has realised that nobody is going to come and meet him, the GRU officers may observe what he does, where he goes after the aborted meeting and what action he takes.

The *secret rendezvous (Yavka)* is often confused with the secret house or *Yavotchnaya Kvartira*. At the present time the term 'secret house' is not used in the GRU. It has been replaced by the term 'secret flat' or KK but the word *Yavka* is used to mean a meeting between two men who are unknown to each other, for example two illegals, or an agent with his new case officer. The secret rendezvous as an element of agent communications is given to all agents without exception – they are given the place, time, recognition signals, password and answer – because the secret rendezvous is essential for re-establishing lost contacts. For example, if in extreme circumstances the whole of the Soviet embassy was declared *persona non grata* and had to leave the country, the agent who had lost contact with his case officer would be obliged to go to a certain place on the 31st of every month which has thirty-one days, that is seven times a year, having previously agreed recognition signals (brief case in left hand, book in right hand, and so on). In the appointed place another person will come towards him and will give the previously arranged password to which the agent gives the proper reply. In giving the correct reply the agent shows to his new leader that he has not made a mistake and secondly that the agent acknowledges the authority of his new case officer. If nobody comes to the pre-arranged place, the agent is obliged to repeat the process until such time as somebody does appear to re-establish contact.

As the agent becomes more and more involved in his work, elements of non-personal contact gradually take the place of personal contact. The most experienced agents have only one element of personal contact – the secret rendezvous or *Yavka* – and several elements of non-personal contact. Let us examine these. First there is the long-range two-way radio link, generally imagined as a special portable radio set which may transmit information directly to the receiving centre on Soviet territory or to a Soviet ship or satellite. This classical element in all spy films is in practice only used in wartime. Instead agents and illegals are issued with small written instructions containing several types of ordinary current components which may be bought in any radio shop, and the means whereby they may be put together to make a long-range two-way set. This solves two problems at the same time. If an agent is arrested there is only to be found in his flat a pair of good Japanese receivers, a tape recorder and other components which can be bought in any shop. There is therefore no way that he can be suspected of any criminal activity. And secondly the problem of the transportation and secret storage of a radio set of comparatively large proportions is avoided. The GRU is continually looking at the market as regards radio sets and components, and working out new recommendations as to how they should be assembled. In times of war, however, quick-acting and ultra-quick-acting sets are used, exploiting technical means of radio transmission in seconds or micro-seconds. Satellites are used in conjunction with these sets and this makes it possible to transmit information on a narrow radio beam vertically overhead. The long-range one-way radio link does not replace, but augments the two-way link. The most convenient, reliable and secure type of link is inevitably the one by which the agent receives from the Centre. One-way radio links are usually broadcast by Soviet radio stations or special ships or polar stations to be received anywhere in the world by ordinary radio receivers. Instructions to the agent are transmitted in the form of previously agreed phrases or numbers in ordinary radio programmes, or as a simple numerical code. Even if a police force should by some means or another guess that the transmission they are hearing is not a coded transmission for cosmonauts or warships, they cannot possibly determine for which spy it is destined, or even which country. The agent who hears such a transmission is also not exposed to any great risk. However, for the GRU it is often necessary that the agent himself transmits. For this the short-range radio link exists. The agent transmits information to the Soviet embassy with the help of small transmitters, like the sort of walkie-talkie sets which can be bought in any shop and which are used for guiding model aeroplanes and ships (one cannot help noticing how many aerials there are on the roof of the Soviet embassy). In this type of radio exchange the GRU takes the cover of a fireman, ambulance driver, construction worker or a policeman. All radio conversations within the city limits are thoroughly studied by GRU specialists and any of them may be used by the GRU for its dark ends. A short-range special link is an alternative to short-range radio links. In connection with increasing the monitoring of radio exchanges, the GRU frequently undertakes the transmission of signals under water. One fisherman will transmit signals by means of a rod put in the water and another several kilometres distant from him will receive the signal by using the same method. Or water and gas pipes can be used. Significant research is also going on in the field of electro-optical communications.

Dead-letter boxes are the favourite GRU means of contact. They have the most universal application and in addition to communications they may be used for the storage of everything that has to do with a spy's work – documents, money, radio sets, special photographic equipment, for example. Thousands of types of dead-letter boxes are known, from cracks in gravestones and brickwork to specially devised magnetic 'letter boxes' in the form of metal nuts. Applied to the structure of a bridge among thousands of similar nuts and rivets this device is easily hidden and just as easy to undo. The GRU also makes wide use of boxes constructed in the form of a plastic hollow wedge with a lid. These can very easily be pushed into the ground in any public park. Underwater dead-letter boxes are also widely used.

Their selection is always a complicated and responsible business. The primary criterion is that as far as possible they must not be prone to accidental discovery. They are threatened by many possible happenings: they may be found by children, by the police, even by archaeologists. There may be floods, or the heat of summer may affect them. Someone may start building on the site. All this must be taken into account. Equally important is that the dead-letter box's location must be easy to describe to another person, even by somebody who only knows about it at secondhand. It must also be located in a place where it is possible for the case officer to go at any time with a plausible cover story for his presence there. Some random examples from GRU practice are worth describing.

As a general principle of security, each dead-letter box (DLB) may only be used once. Documents on all DLBs are stored in the GRU command point and after the completion of a DLB operation the document is stamped 'used' and transferred to the archives. An officer at a command point, working in a GRU top secret archive, once discovered the description of a DLB on which there was no 'used' stamp. The document was very old, pre-war. The DLB has been selected in 1932 and three years later some material had been put in it – money and valuables for the use of the illegal residency in case of emergency, apparently 'in various currencies to a total sum of 50,000 American dollars'. The officer carefully inspected the document again, but there was nothing on it to show that the DLB had been emptied. The officer informed his chief of what he had found and he in his turn informed the GRU chief, who decided on an investigation. The affair was not complicated and a week later the investigation disclosed that the dead-letter box had belonged to the Hamburg illegal residency which in 1937 had been recalled to Moscow lock, stock and barrel for 'instructions', and shot. All the materials of the residency had been handed in to the archives, together with the document about the unused DLB. The new officers who took the place of those who had been shot were completely inexperienced and started work with new sets of documents. There was no time, in any case, to look into the old documents. Then the new GRU staff was also liquidated. So there were many documents which were completely forgotten and simply collected dust in the archives.

The GRU chief took two decisions, firstly, to nominate a group of specially trusted officers for permanent archive work – perhaps something else of interest might be discovered – and secondly, to give an order to one of the GRU residencies in West Germany to find this old unused DLB. Suppose it was still there. If it was, then the value of its contents would have increased many times.

In fact the DLB *had* survived, in spite of the war, the fierce bombing of Hamburg, the rebuilding of the city after the war, and the enormous expansion in the development of the city. The DLB consisted of a hermetically sealed container, about the size of a small suitcase, which had been buried at the bottom of a lake in a quiet park. For greater security it had been covered with an old tombstone which had been sprinkled all over with sand and silt. The container was removed to Moscow and opened there. Much to the disappointment of all those present, all that was inside was a few dozen old-fashioned silver watches of very little value, a hundred or so American dollars and a few thousand crisp German Marks of the time of the Third Reich.

The second dead-letter box was in the very centre of the American capital. At the beginning of his lunch break, the agent would go into a park and hide top secret documents in the hollow of a tree. Some minutes later a Soviet 'diplomat' would appear, remove the documents and with the help of two other 'diplomats' copy them in his car which was parked at the Capitol. The operation was an especially daring one, and succeeded several times—after the GRU chief had sanctioned repeated use of the DLB. The copying of the documents in the car did not take more than twenty minutes, and the agent, on his return from his lunch break, was able to walk in the park for a few minutes longer and retrieve his documents. One day the case officer was making his way towards the dead-letter box. Suddenly his attention was attracted by a sheet of white paper blowing about with the first yellow and red leaves. The officer picked it up and, horrified, saw the stamp 'top secret'. He looked around. All over the park were dozens of similar sheets of paper. The officer realised that squirrels getting ready for winter had taken up residence in the hollowed-out tree; the pieces of paper had got in their way and they had thrown them out. He immediately set about picking up the pieces, many of which were torn by the sharp teeth and claws of these lovable little animals. At that dramatic moment a policeman appeared in the park. He evidently took the Soviet diplomat for one of the White House workers who had had his papers blown out of his hands by the wind. Without a word, the policeman also started to collect the papers. Having gathered a considerable number, the policeman held them out to the embarrassed case officer. The latter took them and smiled in the most foolish way, even forgetting to thank his saviour and helper, who saluted and withdrew. Nevertheless the situation remained highly critical. There was absolutely no time, as the agent had already appeared on the opposite side of the park. The case officer hurried to meet him, although this was strictly forbidden. Quickly outlining the situation, the officer suggested two possible ways out: either the agent should tell his department that he had in error torn up the papers and thrown them into the waste-paper basket but then had remembered in time; or he should wait for four days. The agent chose the second option. Within hours, an officer with diplomatic rank had made two changes of aircraft in Europe and arrived in Warsaw where a fast fighter interceptor was waiting for him. Again only hours later, the GRU had carried out a complete forgery of the documents, and a day later they were returned to the agent. Of course, all this time he had been threatened with exposure, but the GRU's swift action had saved him.

A third dead-letter box was in a small drainage pipe on the embankment of a river in northern Europe. The officer had to lower into the pipe a small metal box with a magnet attached. The magnet was very strong and normally there would have been no risk that the box would come unstuck. Pretending to tie up his shoe-lace, the officer carefully lowered the little box into the drainage pipe with the magnet and took out his hand. But the first frosts had started and the officer had not taken into account the fact that the interior of the pipe was covered with a thin layer of ice. The box slid down the pipe, giving out a harmonious ringing noise, and after a few seconds flew out into the river, which was unfortunately also covered with a thin sheet of ice. Had the river not been iced over, the box would have sunk and that would have been that. But instead it skidded on the ice right to the middle of the river. The ice was too thin to walk on, and nor was it possible to throw things at the box across the ice to send it to the other side. In the box was a film with instructions for an agent. There was only one way out. The officer ran into a shop and bought a fishing rod; then, for an hour and a half, to the astonishment of passers-by, he cast his hook onto the ice until it was taken by the magnet. By carefully winding in his line, he succeeded in retrieving the valuable box. This happened in the heart of one of the Western capitals in broad daylight.

Signals, too, are a means of exchanging information which is highly favoured by the GRU. Office pins are used as signals stuck in a predetermined place, dots, bands, crosses, signals are made with chalk, pencil, paints, lipstick. A car parked in a pre-arranged place at a pre-arranged time may serve as a signal or a doll placed in a window of a house. These are used as warnings of danger, requests for meetings, confirmation of the reception of radio instructions and for hundreds of other intentions.

Usually an agent who has worked for some years with the GRU will have as a minimum the following elements of communication: the secret rendezvous, long-range one-way radio link, short-range radio line or special link and a system of dead-letter boxes and signals. An agent group in addition is obliged in every case to have a long-range two-way radio link.

Chapter Six

The Practice of Agent Work

So our agent has been recruited, trained during long routine meetings (perhaps in a small hotel off the beaten track), and there has been worked out for him a complicated system of agent communications including both personal and non-personal forms of communication and also the actions to be taken in case of a sudden break of all channels of communication. Elements of non-personal communication have been gradually introduced and have gradually superseded the personal meetings. In these meetings the agent has handed over photocopies of secret documents and has received in exchange small sums of money. Attempts by the agent to protest or refuse to work have been successfully suppressed. The material received from him has been thoroughly compared and checked with analogous material received from other sources. So far, all is going well. What happens next is a new stage, the thinking behind which includes the segregation of the agent from the Soviet embassy and from all meetings with official Soviet representatives.

Up till the Second World War not only the agents of under-cover residencies, but also illegals and agents subordinate to illegals, were tied to the embassies. With the outbreak of war, when the embassies were closed, all contact with the powerful agent network was lost. The flow of agent information was cut off at the very moment when it would have been of the greatest value. The deputy head of the GRU was sent into occupied Europe with several radio officers and unlimited powers. Within a short time he had successfully organised a small illegal resident network on the territories of Belgium and Holland. Subsequently, by means of secret rendezvous, he was able to re-establish contact with all the illegal residencies. However, the agent radio station by the name of 'Sever', which had been established before the war, proved useless. Nobody had supposed that the advance of the Nazis would be so precipitate, and the radio station had not been designed to deal with such long distances. The ships of the Soviet Baltic fleet were blockaded in their own bases and could not be used for the reception of agent transmissions. Then the GRU organised a receiving centre on the territory of the Soviet embassy in Sweden. Information from all the illegal residencies came to the illegal residency network and from there was transmitted directly to the Soviet Union. This was perhaps the only possible solution at the time and of course it had many disadvantages. First of all, the agents, their case officers and the illegals found themselves in one gigantic residency, a state of affairs which compromised many hundreds of men. It could not be long before it collapsed, and the collapse began in the most vulnerable place, deep in the nerve centre of this most unprecedently powerful underground organisation. One of the illegal radio operators, wishing to obtain the favours of a girl, boasted to her that he knew all the latest news in the world, as he regularly listened to the radio (which was, of course, forbidden on occupied territory). The girl, in her turn eager for the favours of a certain German corporal, informed him of this fact. So the most powerful underground intelligence organisation in history was discovered – this organisation which had penetrated many of Germany's most sensitive secrets. Referred to by the Germans as 'the Red Orchestra', the organisation was completely neutralised and all the agents and illegals of this gigantic octopus arrested.

The GRU learnt its lessons very quickly. Already, only a few months after what had happened, illegal residencies were functioning on the territories of its true 'allies', the United States, Great Britain and Canada which were completely separate from the embassies. This now cast-iron rule is observed by the GRU everywhere. Undercover residencies support illegals, but only on instructions from the Centre without having any idea for whom they are working. All operations in support of illegals are worked out in such a way that the officers of the GRU undercover residency do not have one crumb of information which is not necessary. Operations are planned in such a way that there is no possibility of the illegals becoming dependent on the actions of the undercover residency. Another lesson learnt from the arrest of the 'Red Orchestra' is the division of residencies into even smaller independent parts, especially insofar as this concerns illegals. And, thirdly and significantly, there is the separation of agents from the embassy which is our present concern.

The recruited, tested and trained agent *must* be kept separate from official Soviet institutions abroad. The process of separating the agent is undertaken only after he has handed over to the GRU a significant quantity of secret material, that is, made it impossible for himself to go to the police. The separated agent comes in three guises: the separated acting agent, the agent group and the agent residency.

The most valuable agents, those that provide specially important material, are taken out of residencies very quickly. The moment the Centre feels that such and such an agent is handing over material of exceptional importance, it will immediately demand that no more information or documents are taken from him. All attention is switched from questions of obtaining information to questions of security and training. The GRU will then take the step of sending him immediately to a soft country to undergo his training there – during a 'holiday', perhaps. If circumstances permit, he may be transferred from the soft country to the Soviet Union. Thence he will go back to his own country, but as an independently acting agent. He will be run exclusively by the Centre, in concrete terms the head of a section, even, in special cases, the head of a directorate and in extreme cases the deputy head of the GRU or the head himself. The running of such an agent is thus carried out exactly as the running of illegals is.

A complex system of non-personal communications and contacts must be worked out for an independent agent. Usually he will transmit his material by means of dead-letter boxes. The residency which was responsible for the agent's recruitment may receive the order to empty such and such a numbered dead-letter box of films. It will not know from whom it is receiving these films, whether from a local illegal or a transiting illegal, an 'artist on tour' as they are still called, or from an agent who has been recruited by that particular residency. The processing of films (which are called *schtchit* – the Russian word for shield) is carried out only in the Centre. The film will be a dual-purpose one. Firstly a pseudo-secret document is photographed on the film by the GRU, then the film is given to the agent and he photographs genuine secret material on it. Any attempt to develop the film outside the walls of the GRU Technical Operations Scientific Research Institute leads to the real secret text being destroyed and only the pseudo-secret text appearing, which is designed to lead the police on a wild goose chase.

The Scientific Research Institute of the GRU has done much important work in developing films of the *schtchit* type. Hundreds, or even possibly thousands, of formulae have been worked out. In each case, for each and every valuable agent, a separate and unrepeatable formula is used. The GRU tries by all possible means to limit the number of personal contacts with independent agents, which is why they are taken out of the residencies. If personal meetings have to take place, they are only carried out in soft countries or secretly in the Soviet Union. In any case, they are carried out extremely rarely.

Other agents recruited by residencies are gradually organised into agent groups of three to five men each. Usually, agents working in one particular field of espionage are put together in one group. Sometimes a group consists of agents who for various reasons are known to each other. Let us suppose that one agent recruits two others. A group automatically organises itself. The GRU obviously considers family groups containing the head of the family and his wife and children to be more secure and stable. The members of such a group may work in completely different fields of espionage. The leader of an agent group is called a *gropovod*, and only he is in contact with Soviet officers. Thus to a certain extent the members of agent groups are completely isolated from Soviet diplomatic representation. The agent group is in contact with the undercover residency for a period of time, then gradually the system of contact with the residency comes to an end and orders begin to be received directly from Moscow. By various channels the group sends it material directly to Moscow. Finally the contact with Moscow becomes permanent and stable and the agent group is entirely separated from the residency. With gradual changes in personnel at the residency, like the resident himself, the cipher officers and the operational officers with whom there was once direct contact, nobody outside the Centre will know of the existence of this particular group. Should it happen that operating conditions become difficult, or that the embassy is blockaded or closed down, the group will be able to continue its activities in the same way as before.

The GRU tolerates personal contacts with group leaders only in exceptional circumstances and where there is favourable security. Agents going into agent groups do not by any means always know each other, nor is it necessary that they should. They may know the group leader alone, not guessing at the existence of other agents.

An agent group may gradually get bigger as the group leader or his recruiting agent continues to recruit other agents. If the Centre permits a group leader to recruit agents independently, his agent group, even if it consists of only two men, acquires the status of an agent residency, and the group leader becomes the agent resident. This status was acquired by one of the American nuclear physicists whom the GRU permitted to recruit his colleagues at his discretion. Interestingly this agent resident never made a mistake.

Sometimes the GRU will post one or more illegals to an agent residency. The presence of even one Soviet illegal (he is of course considered as the leader) in an agent residency of any size automatically transforms that residency from an agent residency into an illegal residency. This process of increasing the numbers and the gradual self-generation of independent organisations continues endlessly. The process is similar to the spread of a fearful illness, with the difference that, in this case, surgical intervention always gives excellent results. Hundreds of examples have proved this.

If the GRU feels that there is likely to be a clampdown and that operating conditions will become more difficult at any moment, it takes measures to ensure that it does not lose the agent network which has already been recruited but not as yet separated from the undercover residency. With this aim in mind some of the most experienced officers of the undercover residency are in a continual state of readiness so that at any moment, on the order of the Centre, they may go over to illegal status and run the work of their agents. These officers are in possession of previously prepared documents and equipment, and gold, diamonds and other valuables which will be of use to them in their illegal activities will have been hidden in secret hiding-places beforehand. In case of war actually breaking out, these officers will unobtrusively disappear from their embassies. The Soviet government will register a protest and will for a short time refuse to exchange its diplomats for the diplomats of the aggressive country. Then it will capitulate, the exchange will take place and the newly fledged illegals will remain behind in safe houses and flats. Afterwards they will gradually, by using the system of secret rendezvous, begin to establish the system of contacts with agents and agent groups which have recently been subordinated to the undercover residency. Now they all form a new illegal residency. The new illegals never mix and never enter into contact with the old ones who have been working in the country for a long time. This plainly makes life more secure for both parties. The formation of new illegal residencies where there were already old ones in action is yet another example of the constant striving for duplication.

However important the problems of recruiting agents, training them and organising agent networks may be, there is still one overriding objective: the acquisition of secrets belonging to an enemy or a probable enemy. The material acquired by the GRU breaks down into information, documents and specimens or samples. Information includes commentaries and reports. Documents are not the subjective opinions or observations of agents but official secret papers, books, drawings or copies of them. Specimens or samples are self-explanatory: actual weapons, examples of military technology, instruments and equipment which the GRU uses for study and copying.

The photographing of documents and eavesdropping on conversations are in real life exactly as they are portrayed in spy films. But how does the agent contrive to steal secret equipment and remain undetected? Many ways and means exist: we have already examined one of them when we discussed the recruitment of the owners of small private companies producing military equipment. The owner of a small firm has not much difficulty in producing one extra specimen of an instrument or a gadget and it is very advantageous for him to sell it to the GRU. But what about really big objects like a tank, an aeroplane or an atomic reactor? Not only does one have to obtain such an object without its loss being noticed, but it also has to be transported to the Soviet Union. There is, perhaps surprisingly, a number of solutions to these problems. Samples of objects which can only be used once — rockets, torpedoes, shells, cartridges — are usually stolen during instructional periods, military displays or tests. An entry may be made, for example, in the official accounting documents that there were a hundred launchings of a certain anti-tank rocket whereas in actual fact there were only ninety-nine. The hundredth rocket will have been quietly sold to the GRU without anybody noticing. Very often written-off equipment is able to be sold because there exist official documents certifying that it has been written off or destroyed. One agent suggested to the GRU that he should obtain for them a lateral scanning radar for aircraft which permitted the aircraft to carry out intelligence work on the territory of the enemy while it was actually over its own territory. The GRU, of course, agreed to the suggestion, although the agent said that he did not know exactly when he would be able to acquire the apparatus. It might be within a day or two, it might take years. The GRU agreed to wait. Several months later the agent obtained the apparatus, and a year later it was taken into service with the Soviet Army. The agent worked in an experimental training ground, and when an aircraft equipped with the required apparatus crashed, the agent, in spite of very strict control, was able to steal a broken radar. This was quite sufficient for the Soviet Army to catch up with the United States in that particular field. Frequently agents go as far as deliberately damaging secret arms and equipment so that they can be written off and then sold. Wide use is made of countries of the Third World which receive equipment from Western countries, as was made clear in the GRU's (unsuccessful) attempt to acquire a French Mirage III from the Lebanon. Any armed conflict or change of government is usually accompanied by intense GRU activity, because this is the most favourable time for stealing military technology and armaments.

The diplomatic mail is the most often-used method of transporting specimens to the Soviet Union. The main problem is to transport the specimen into the Soviet embassy. From that time onwards, of course, it crosses all frontiers in sealed packing cases and accompanied by armed diplomatic couriers. Sometimes the difficult problem arises of a specimen weighing several tons which cannot be accommodated in the diplomatic post. This happened when, in one of the countries which had bought Leopard tanks in the Federal Republic of Germany, GRU agents were able to steal a written-off tank engine – an item of exceptional interest to Soviet industry. The theft went unnoticed but the engine weighed more than a ton and there was no way it could

134

be accommodated in diplomatic containers. The Soviet consulate then bought an old cruising yacht. The yacht was straight away sent for a refit and, for a very substantial sum, the small repair workshop installed the heavy tank engine in the yacht. The yacht went to sea on a number of pleasure trips and during one such trip fortuitously met a Soviet trawler. A special team of fitters literally tore the tank engine out of the yacht in a few minutes. The yacht put to sea several times after this to maintain its cover, before being sold.

Another, more reliable method of transporting heavy equipment exists. After an item has been acquired, GRU officers in the guise of a trade delegation will poach from a firm some completely unnecessary item of quite innocent nature. The important thing is that the quantity of containers and their weight approximate to the packing of the secret equipment. Subsequently the markings on the packing cases are changed and they make their way innocently through customs control. So items of exceptional importance are transported to the Soviet Union in the form of equipment for, say, a canning factory. Sometimes, too, specimens are sent to a safe address in one of the Third World countries where they can be loaded onto Soviet ships without any trouble.

In general terms the GRU leadership is quite confident that it is capable of obtaining any technological secret from the West provided it has been allocated a sufficient sum of money. Only one technological secret exists which the GRU is incapable of obtaining. Even if it did obtain it, the Soviet system would not be able to copy it since for that, the whole structure of communism would have to be changed. Yet this technological secret is of vital importance to the Soviet system. It is the Achilles' heel of socialism — strike at it and socialism will fall to pieces, all invasion, nationalisation and collectivisation will cease. This secret is nothing more than the means of producing bread. Socialism, for all its gigantic resources, is not capable of feeding itself. How easy it would be, one sometimes thinks, to place an embargo on the supply of bread to the Soviet Union, until Soviet forces no longer found themselves in occupied Czechoslovakia, Lithuania, Estonia and Latvia, until such time as the Cubans no longer held sway in Africa, until the Berlin Wall disappeared. It would only be necessary to withhold supplies of grain for a few months, and the whole edifice of socialism might fall to pieces.

Chapter Seven

Operational Intelligence

Operational intelligence marks a complete departure from the kind we have talked about until now. It embraces intelligence organisations subordinated to operational units – fronts, fleets, groups of forces, military districts, armies, flotillas – whose job is to aid in the implementation of the military activity. Organisationally, the Soviet Army consists of sixteen military districts and four groups of forces in Germany, Poland, Czechoslovakia and Hungary. In war, or at the time of preparations for war, the groups of forces and military districts are transformed into fronts and army groups. Each military district, groups of forces and front has a staff, each with its own intelligence directorate (called RU or Second Directorate of the Military District Staff). The chief of the Second Directorate of the Military District Staff is the chief of all intelligence units of the military district. He is officially called the head of military district intelligence. All twenty heads of military district intelligence and groups of forces are under the command of the head of the GRU Fifth Directorate. The GRU Fifth Directorate supervises the activity of the intelligence directorates, carries out the posting of senior officers of operational intelligence, collates the work experience of all operational intelligence and issues corresponding recommendations and instructions. In addition, the head of intelligence is subordinated to the chief of the military district staff. The chief of staff directs the daily activity of the head of intelligence. The head of intelligence of a military district works exclusively in the interests of his military district, in conformity with the orders of the chief of staff and the commander of the military district. At the same time, all information obtained is forwarded to the GRU too. The role the GRU plays is to collect information from all heads of intelligence and forward to them information obtained by other intelligence organs. Sometimes, the intelligence directorate of the military district may work directly in the interests of the GRU but this must be done only with the agreement of the military district commander. The chief of the general staff is the supreme arbiter in disputes between the commander of the military district and the head of the GRU. However, in practice such disputes occur extremely rarely.

Each front, group of forces and military district consists of armies. Normally a front has an air force, a tank army and two to three all-arms armies. Each army consists of four to seven divisions. Sometimes a corps is included – two to three divisions. Each army and corps has a staff, among whose members is an intelligence section which is called RO* or Army Staff Second Department. The head of the army intelligence section is the head of all intelligence units belonging to a given army. He also ranks below two other officers: the chief of staff of his army, and the chief of intelligence of the military district.

His relationship with his chiefs is based on similar lines. He works exclusively in the interests of his army, obeying the orders of the army commander and the army chief of staff. At the same time, all information acquired by him is also forwarded to the intelligence chief of the military district. A reciprocal arrangement exists whereby the intelligence chief of the military district forwards information to his heads of army intelligence which he has received from other armies, the intelligence directorates of the military districts and the GRU.

The Soviet navy consists of four fleets, the Northern, Pacific, Black Sea and Baltic fleets. Each of the fleets is the equal of a military district, group of forces, and front, and has a staff which includes an intelligence directorate or Naval Staff Second Directorate. Its head is the chief of Naval Intelligence. The naval directorates have the same organisation as those in military districts, fronts and groups of forces. The difference lies in the fact that while the army directorates are subordinated directly to the Fifth Directorate of the GRU, the four naval directorates fall under an organisation called naval intelligence. In its turn naval intelligence comes under the head of the GRU and is controlled by the Fifth Directorate. The reason for this extra organisational step is that ships of all four fleets frequently operate in all oceans as

* *Razvedyvatelnyi otdel*

4. Operational Intelligence

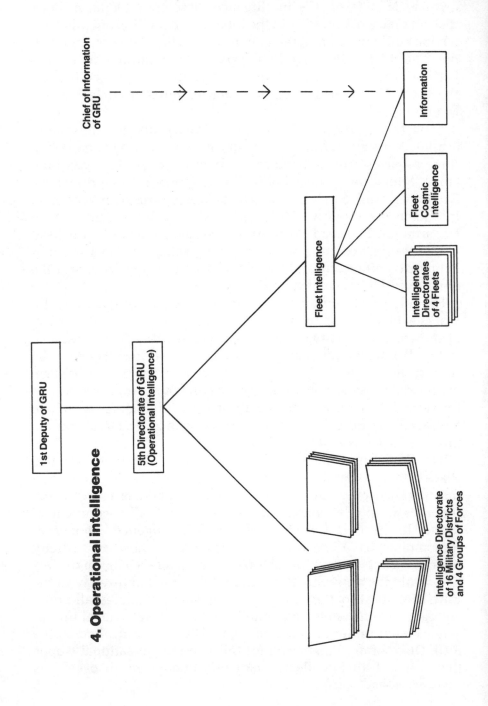

1st Deputy of GRU

5th Directorate of GRU (Operational Intelligence)

Chief of Information of GRU

Fleet Intelligence

Information

Fleet Cosmic Intelligence

Intelligence Directorates of 4 Fleets

Intelligence Directorate of 16 Military Districts and 4 Groups of Forces combined squadrons. For this reason the ships need information, not about a narrow sector like the troops of a military district, but on a much wider scale.

Naval intelligence was created to co-ordinate naval information from every ocean of the world, and is a component of the High Staff of the Navy of the USSR. In addition to its normal powerful apparatus for gathering information, there is also the naval cosmic intelligence department. The Soviet Union therefore possesses two independent cosmic intelligence organisations, the GRU's own and the Navy's cosmic intelligence organisation. Although naval cosmic intelligence works in the interests of the High Commander of the Soviet Navy, all information from it is handed over to the GRU. The co-operation between the two cosmic services is co-ordinated by the chief of the General Staff. Should a very serious situation arise, the same task may be set at the same time to both services and the results arrived at then collated and compared.

The organisation of intelligence directorates (RUs) on the staffs of military districts, groups of forces, fronts and fleets is standardised. The intelligence directorate consists of five departments and two groups:

First Department or Department of Reconnaissance directs the activities of the reconnaissance units of the tactical wing, that is, reconnaissance battalions of divisions and reconnaissance companies of regiments. In naval terminology this department is called the *Ship Reconnaissance Department*. It directs the collection of information which comes directly from serving surface vessels and submarines at sea, bearing in mind that what is meant here are normal warships and not special intelligence collecting ships. The training of officers of First Departments is carried out in the intelligence faculty of the Frunze Military Academy and the corresponding faculty of the Naval Academy. The officers of First Departments are usually experienced army and navy officers who have considerable experience of service in reconnaissance units.

Second Department or Department of Agent Intelligence is concerned with the recruitment of secret agents and the obtaining through them of intelligence information of interest to the staff.

139

The recruitment of agents and the creation of agent networks is carried out on the territories of contiguous countries where the military district concerned would expect to operate in war-time. Naval Intelligence is interested in recruiting agents from all territories, especially in large ports and naval bases. An intelligence centre and three or four intelligence points are subordinated to the Second Department which is directly concerned with agent work.

The centre is concerned with the recruitment of agents in the contiguous state, whereas the intelligence points only recruit agents in specific sectors and areas. They work independently from one another, although they are co-ordinated by the chief of the Second Department. The training of officers for work in the Second Departments and also in centres and points is carried out by the Third Faculty of the Military-Diplomatic Academy (the Academy of the Soviet Army).

The Third Department or Spetsnaz Department is concerned with the preparation and carrying out of diversionary acts on enemy territory, the liquidation of political and military leaders, the destruction of lines of communication and supply and the carrying out of terrorist operations with the aim of undermining the enemy's will to continue fighting. A *Spetsnaz* intelligence point is subordinated to this department and this carries out the recruitment of agent-terrorists on the territory of any possible future enemy. There is also a *Spetsnaz* brigade which consists of 1,300 cut-throat soldiers. The officers who work in the *Spetsnaz* intelligence points and those who direct their activities in the Third Department are trained, rather incongruously, in the Third Faculty of the Military-Diplomatic Academy, although for the *Spetsnaz* brigade and the officers connected with it training takes place in the Frunze Academy. Analogous organisations can be seen in the Navy, with this difference: the brigades are called *Spetsnaz* naval brigades (not to be confused with Naval infantry brigades) and the same 'diplomats' direct the activity of all agent-assassins in the fleets.

The Fourth Department or Information Department carries out the collection and collation of all intelligence coming into the intelligence directorate.

The *Fifth Department* is occupied with electronic intelligence, and this department directs two regiments, the Radio Intelligence Regiment and the Radio-Technical Intelligence Regiment. Radio Intelligence carries out the interception of radio signals and Radio-Technical Intelligence is concerned with tracking emissions from the enemy's radar.

The *Intelligence Directorate Technical Facilities Group* is occupied with the interpretation of air photographs. The training of specialists for such work is carried on at the Second Kharkov Higher Military Aviation and Engineering School.

The *Interpreters' Group* or 'the Inquisition' deals with the deciphering and translation of documents obtained, and with the interrogation of prisoners of war. Specialists for this group are prepared at the Military Institute (of Foreign Languages).

The Intelligence Department of the Army Staff
This may be seen as an intelligence directorate in miniature. It has very similar organisation: *First Group or Reconnaissance Group*: analogous to the First Department of an Intelligence Directorate and concerned with directing tactical reconnaissance, the difference being that it is only responsible for the divisions of one army, whereas the First Department of an Intelligence Directorate is responsible for all the divisions of its military district; *Second Group or Secret Intelligence Group*; *Third Group or Spetsnaz Group*: responsible for terrorist acts in the area of operations of its army – a specialist company of 115 cut-throat soldiers is part of it; *Fourth Group – Informational*; *Fifth Group* which commands two battalions, radio intelligence and radio-technical intelligence – the Intelligence Department likewise has its own interpreters.

It would be a mistake to think that operational agent intelligence is a kind of second-class citizen compared with strategic intelligence. Every intelligence directorate is a kind of GRU in miniature with its electronic facilities, information services, secret agents and even, where the fleet is concerned, its independent cosmic service. During the course of a war, or immediately before war breaks out, the power of an intelligence directorate is immeasurably increased by the infiltration in the

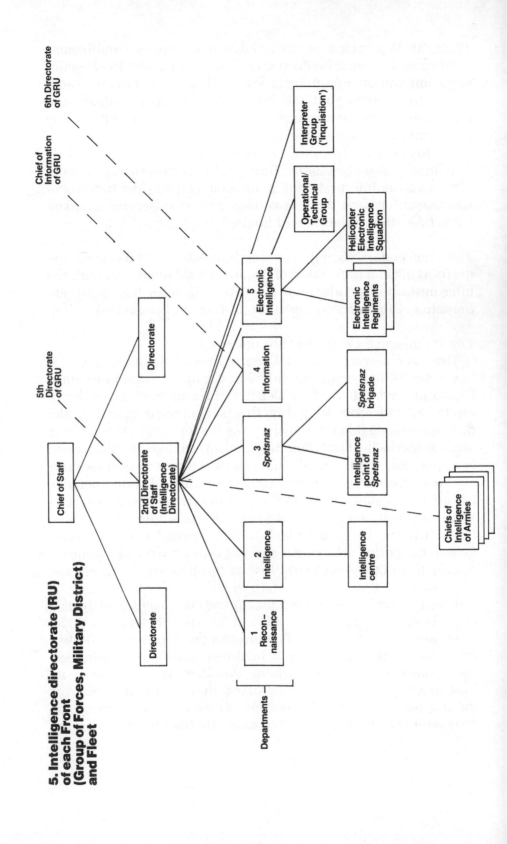

5. Intelligence directorate (RU) of each Front (Group of Forces, Military District) and Fleet

Chief of Staff

5th Directorate of GRU

Chief of Information of GRU

6th Directorate of GRU

Directorate

2nd Directorate of Staff (Intelligence Directorate)

Directorate

1 Recon-naissance

2 Intelligence

3 Spetsnaz

4 Information

5 Electronic Intelligence

Departments

Intelligence centre

Intelligence point of Spetsnaz

Spetsnaz brigade

Electronic Intelligence Regiments

Helicopter Electronic Intelligence Squadron

Operational/ Technical Group

Interpreter Group ('Inquisition')

Chiefs of Intelligence of Armies

enemy's rear of thousands of *Spetsnaz* saboteurs. The intelligence directorates taken altogether form a very powerful intelligence conglomerate, in no way inferior in its scope to strategic intelligence. In other words the GRU, in the form of strategic and operational intelligence, has created two agent networks independent of one another and each duplicating the other. In countries like Norway, Sweden, West Germany, Austria, Turkey, Afghanistan and China the operational intelligence agent network by far exceeds strategic intelligence in strength, effectiveness and invulnerability. This can be confirmed by examining the task of the different intelligence directorates:

Northern Fleet – covering Norway, Great Britain, France, Spain, Portugal, Canada and the USA. There is no doubt that Northern Fleet intelligence is mainly restricted to targets on the sea shore or coastline, although this certainly does not preclude deep agent penetration of the whole territory of the country being investigated, including the central government organs.

Baltic Fleet – covering Sweden, Denmark, West Germany.

Black Sea Fleet – covering Turkey and the whole Mediterranean coastline.

Pacific Fleet – covering the USA, Japan, China, Canada and all countries of the Pacific Basin.

Leningrad Military District – Norway and Sweden. Agent intelligence work is not carried out on Finnish territory, since this country is well inside the Soviet sphere of influence, and its behaviour pleases the Kremlin much more than that of certain Warsaw pact countries, for example, Romania.

Baltic Military District – Sweden, Denmark.

Soviet Groups of Forces in Germany, the Northern Group of Forces in Poland, the Byelorussian Military District – all are concerned with the study of the German Federal Republic.

Central Group of Forces in Czechoslovakia – covering the German Federal Republic and Austria.

Southern Group of Forces in Hungary – Austria.

Carpathian Military District – covering Greece and Turkey from Bulgarian territory.

Kiev and Odessa Military District – Turkey, Austria.

Trans-Caucasian Military District – Turkey, Iran.

Turkestan Military District – Iran, Afghanistan.

Mid-Asian Military District – Afghanistan, China.
Trans-Baikal and Far Eastern Military Districts – China.
Moscow, Northern Caucasian, Volga, Ural and Siberian Military Districts – these do not run agent networks in peace time.

Taking two countries, West Germany and Turkey, as examples, let us analyse the strengths and facilities of strategic and operational intelligence networks and likewise the KGB networks:

West Germany has been infiltrated by: the GRU strategic agent network; several illegal residencies and agent groups; five undercover residencies in Bonn and Cologne, and three Soviet-controlled missions in British, American and French sectors; the Berlin direction of the GRU; it is also covered by the GRU operational agent network. Here, completely independently, work is also carried out by the intelligence directorate of the Baltic Fleet, Soviet troops in Germany, and the Northern and Central groups of forces in the Byelorussian Military District. In other words West Germany is subject to the attentions of: the agent networks of five intelligence centres; fifteen to eighteen intelligence points plus five intelligence points belonging to the *Spetsnaz* group; five *Spetsnaz* brigades and up to fifteen to twenty separate *Spetsnaz* companies belonging to the same organisation which are at full alert to carry out terrorist acts (the total number of cut-throats is up to 8,000 men). This accounts only for GRU activities. The KGB agent network also runs several illegal residencies and agent groups and two undercover residencies in Bonn and Cologne.

Turkey contains a similar proliferation of Soviet espionage: a GRU strategic agent network in the form of an illegal residency and two undercover residencies in Ankara and Istanbul; a GRU operational network in the form of five intelligence centres belonging to the Carpathian, Odessa, Kiev and Trans-Caucasian Military Districts, and the Black Sea fleet; fifteen to twenty intelligence points, plus five *Spetsnaz* intelligence points and a corresponding quantity of *Spetsnaz* brigades. The KGB provides a strategic network (one illegal residency and two undercover residencies); and a KGB operational network. This network is subordinated to the KGB frontier troops.

These two examples provide a blueprint for intelligence activity in many other countries, especially those having common frontiers with the Soviet Union or its satellites.

The basic difference in working methods between strategic and operational intelligence in the GRU is that officers of operational intelligence do not in peace-time work on the territories of target countries. All operations concerning the identification of suitable candidates, their vetting, testing, recruitment, training and all practical work are carried out on the territories within the Eastern bloc or from inside its frontiers. It may be thought that operational intelligence does not have the range and potential of the strategic branch, whose officers mainly work abroad, but this is not so. Without the possibility of recruiting foreigners in their own countries, operational intelligence seeks and finds other ways of establishing the necessary contacts. Its officers exploit every avenue of approach to attract foreigners visiting the Soviet Union and its satellites into their network. Prime attention is paid to students undergoing instruction in Soviet higher educational institutes, and to specialists visiting the Soviet Union as members of delegations. Naval intelligence actively works against sailors from foreign ships calling at Soviet ports, and operational intelligence is equally careful to study the affairs of Soviet and Eastern bloc citizens who have relatives in countries of interest to it.

Operational intelligence is quite unceremonious in using methods of pressurising its candidates, seeing that the recruitment of foreigners is taking place on its own territory. Having recruited one foreigner, the intelligence directorate then uses him for selecting and recruiting other candidates without a Soviet officer taking part. Frequently, one recruitment on Soviet territory is sufficient for the agent who has been recruited to return to his country and recruit several more agents. Contact between agents who have been recruited and their case officers in the Soviet Union is usually carried out by non-personal channels – radio, secret writing, microdots, dead-letter boxes – and couriers are greatly used, too, people like train drivers and conductors, crew members of aircraft and ships and lorry drivers. Personal contact with operational intelligence agents is only carried out on Soviet bloc territory. There exist numerous examples where meetings with agents take place only once every five to seven years, and cases are known where agents have never met their case officer and have never been either on Soviet or satellite territory. A useful example is that of a lorry driver belonging to a large transport company who was recruited by Soviet operational intelligence whilst visiting Czechoslovakia. Subsequently, having returned to his own country, he recruited a friend who worked in an armaments factory and his brother who lived not far from a very large military airport. The lorry driver only occasionally visited eastern Europe and rarely had contact with Soviet officers because there was always a driver's mate with him. However, every time a journey to eastern Europe was planned, he notified his case officers in good time by means of postcards. Postcards with pre-arranged texts were sent to different addresses in the Eastern bloc and every time the driver crossed into Soviet-controlled territory, officers met him either at customs, or in the restaurant or even the lavatory, to give him short instructions and money. The meetings were carried out in the shortest possible time so that the driver's mate would not suspect anything.

The absence of contact with agents outside territory under the control of the Soviet Union gives GRU operational intelligence exceptional advantages. Firstly, it is extremely difficult to unmask and expose such agents; secondly, and perhaps more important, the Soviet officers of operational intelligence have no chance to defect to the West and expose the activities of the agents recruited by them. (In strategic intelligence this occurs quite regularly but we have as yet not one example of it happening amongst operational intelligence officers.)

Yet another important advantage of operational intelligence, and one which gives it exceptional invulnerability, is its diversification. A defecting officer from strategic intelligence can say a lot about the activities of the central apparatus of the GRU, but an officer of the operational network who did succeed in defecting would be able to reveal only one or two intelligence points or centres – and there are more than a hundred of these in the Soviet Army. Each of them is carefully isolated from the others and, to a great extent, camouflaged. Centres and points are mostly found on the premises of military buildings of exceptional importance, and consequently with the maximum possible protection. Even if an officer did succeed in disclosing the true significance of a particular building, he could only say that it was, for example, a store for nuclear weapons or a rocket depot; it would be almost

146

impossible to determine that in addition there was also an intelligence point. Cases are known where intelligence points have been located on the premises of the personal country houses of important generals or the well-guarded premises of punishment battalions (in other words, military prisons). And the diversification of the operational networks in no way indicates the absence of co-ordination. All these organs and organisations are included in a rigid pyramid system headed by the Fifth GRU Directorate (in turn, of course, subject to the head of the GRU). However, in the activities of the intelligence directorates there exists a certain freedom which invariably engenders useful intiative. The GRU central apparatus prefers not to interfere in the daily running of the intelligence directorates provided that they work in a productive manner and toe the line. The GRU will occasionally interfere, in cases where two different directorates have recruited the same agent, although it will always encourage a situation where different intelligence directorates recruit agents for the same target. For example, the intelligence directorate of a group of forces once recruited an agent for an important scientific research target. Unwittingly the intolligence directorate of another group of forces recruited another agent for the same target. Both agents provided almost identical information which was eventually received in Moscow where it was carefully analysed. The moment one of the agents began to provide false information, it was spotted by the Fifth Directorate which demanded that work should stop with one agent and that there should be greater vigilance in the work with the other agent. Independent penetration is, as we know, practised at all levels in the GRU. The head of an intelligence point may check his agents and reveal negative aspects in their work in good time. The heads of intelligence in military districts check the heads of points and centres and the head of the GRU checks his heads of military district intelligence. An illegal agent network may be used to check the agents of the undercover residencies and operational agent networks and vice-versa. Of course nobody suspects that he is engaged in checking somebody else. All anybody knows is that he is procuring material for the GRU.

Spetsnaz intelligence is the sharpest and most effective weapon in the hands of the heads of intelligence directorates or departments. It consists of two elements – Spetsnaz agents and Spetsnaz

6. Intelligence department (RO) of each of the 41 armies of the Soviet Union

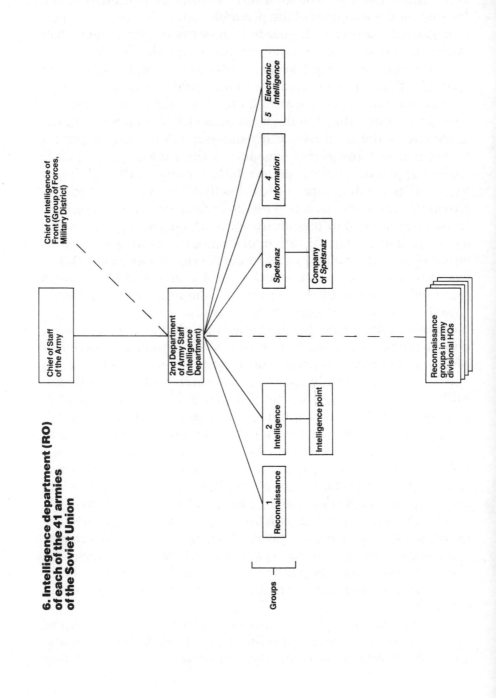

Chief of Intelligence of Front (Group of Forces, Military District)

Chief of Staff of the Army

2nd Department of Army Staff (Intelligence Department)

1 Reconnaissance

2 Intelligence

Intelligence point

3 Spetsnaz

Company of Spetsnaz

4 Information

5 Electronic Intelligence

Groups

Reconnaissance groups in army divisional HQs

detachments. *Spetsnaz* agents are recruited by an intelligence point, and the whole process of recruiting and running agent-saboteurs is identical to the work with ordinary agents of operational intelligence. However, their tasks differ in essence. The basic task of the procurement agent is to provide necessary information. The task of the *Spetsnaz* agent is to carry out terrorist acts. Intelligence directorates try to recruit these agents from within the most important economic and transport targets. On receipt of orders, they must be able and willing to carry out acts of sabotage upon these targets. For the GRU the most important thing is to render unserviceable power and transport targets, electric power stations, electric power lines, oil and gas pipelines, bridges, tunnels and railway equipment. Great stress is placed on carrying out acts of sabotage which will have a strong effect on the morale of the inhabitants over a wide area, such as the blowing up of a large dam or the burning of oil storage tanks. *Spetsnaz* agents form the so-called 'sleeping' agent network which does no work in peace-time but springs into action the moment hostilities break out. Operational intelligence tries to limit its meetings with these agents to exceptional cases.

The *Spetsnaz* detachment is quite different. It is the true élite of the Soviet armed forces. Its members are crack soldiers and officers. On Soviet territory they wear the uniform of airborne troops, on satellite territories they are disguised as auxiliary detachments, normally signals units. (Of course they have no connection with airborne troops or signals. Eight divisions of airborne troops are subject to the commander of airborne forces, who in his turn is answerable only to the Minister of Defence. The airborne forces form a strategic element acting exclusively in the interests of the higher command.) *Spetsnaz* detachments are an organ of the operational field and act in the interests of fronts, fleets and armies. The Soviet Army includes four naval *Spetsnaz* brigades (one to each fleet); sixteen *Spetsnaz* brigades — one to each group of forces and the basic military districts; and forty-one separate companies.

A *Spetsnaz* brigade consists of a headquarters company, three or four airborne battalions and support detachments. In all there are 900 to 1,300 soldiers and officers ready to carry out terrorist operations in the rear of the enemy. A *Spetsnaz* naval brigade is similar, containing a headquarters company, a group of midget

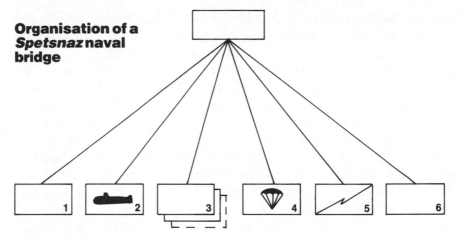

Organisation of a *Spetsnaz* naval bridge

1 – HQ company
2 – Midget submarine group
3 – Combat swimmer battalions
4 – Parachute battalion
5 – Signals company
6 – Supporting units

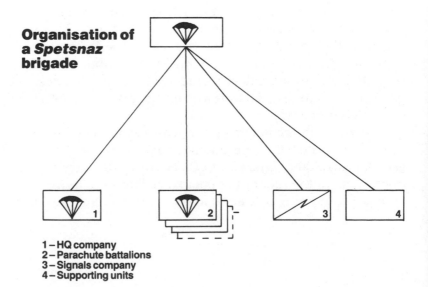

Organisation of a *Spetsnaz* brigade

1 – HQ company
2 – Parachute battalions
3 – Signals company
4 – Supporting units

submarines, a battalion of parachutists and two or three battalions of frogmen. Sometimes the *Spetsnaz* naval brigade is confused with the brigade of the fleet marine infantry, mainly because naval *Spetsnaz* use the uniform of marine infantry to disguise their soldiers and officers. *Spetsnaz* companies in armies and tank armies consist of three platoons of saboteurs and one communications platoon. This means that, all told, there are in peace-time alone 27,000 to 30,000 first-class saboteurs available. During mobilisation this number can be increased by four- or five-fold by recalling reservists who have previously served in these detachments.

The deployment of saboteurs in the enemy's rear is normally carried out by parachute, though in the fleets frogmen also take part. *Spetsnaz* hardly ever use helicopters, because the deployment generally takes place at a considerable distance from the front line. Small groups of *Spetsnaz* brigades are dropped at a depth of 500 to 1,000 kilometres to act in the interests of the frontal forces who will be attacking through areas cleared by atomic action, air attacks and sabotage activities. Simultaneously with the dropping of the front brigade, each army taking part carries out the dropping of its own *Spetsnaz* companies. These are also dropped in small groups, a maximum of fifteen consisting of five or six men each, at depths of 100 to 500 kilometres. There are usually three or four armies and one tank army in each front, so in the course of an attack at a frontal level there are one brigade and four or five separate companies operating at a depth from 100 to 1,000 kilometres in the rear of the enemy. In other words around 250 groups totalling 1,500 to 1,700 men. It must be added that, on West German territory for example, preparations are in hand for not one, but four or five fronts to operate. At the same time the *Spetsnaz* agents are activated.

The *Spetsnaz* detachments have two basic duties: the destruction of the system of the State government and its armies, that is the destruction of staff, command points, networks and lines of communication; and the destruction of nuclear weapons and the means of supplying them – attacks on depots and stores of nuclear weaponry and rockets, aerodromes, rocket launchers and launching pads. Simultaneously with these two basic tasks, the *Spetsnaz* detachments strive to disorganise the internal life of the State and Army and to sow uncertainty and panic.

In carrying out the first task, the leading role is allocated to the staff companies of the *Spetsnaz* brigades. These companies differ from other detachments of *Spetsnaz* in that they are not manned by soldiers who are serving their time, but by professional men, 'ensigns'. These *Spetsnaz* staff companies are specially trained for the kidnapping or destruction of State leaders of the enemy, members of the government and senior military commanders. Their existence is cloaked in the very strictest secrecy. Frequently, many officers and sergeants of *Spetsnaz* brigades do not even suspect the existence of such companies in their brigades. They are kept apart from the normal brigade and camouflaged as parachutists, boxers, wrestlers, unarmed combat experts, marksmen, even sports teams of the military district. The staff company of the *Spetsnaz* brigade is the only unit which carries out its tasks not in camouflaged uniform but in civilian clothes or in the military or police uniform of the enemy. These companies are also the only ones amongst the *Spetsnaz* detachments which, in the course of military operations, may establish contact and act together with the agent-saboteurs of *Spetsnaz*. All the remaining units of saboteurs undertake night flights, mine-laying and the seizure of prisoners in order to obtain information. Tanks and other armoured fighting vehicles (AFVs) belonging to the enemy are of special interest for saboteurs, and all groups have the task of making sudden attacks on AFVs with the aim of stealing them for future use in attacks against given targets. Several groups may take part in an attack on a certain target, and after the attack they will disperse and go their own ways. There is a constant alternation between the collecting of information and the carrying out of sabotage acts. A group may collect information on enemy troop movements in a certain region and transmit the information to its staff, then it may destroy a rocket launcher in another area, then go on to collect more information on troop movements. Everything depends on the tasks set to the group and the initiative of the group commander. When prisoners are taken, the saboteurs know no laws or humanity in their methods of interrogation; nobody who has been in any way connected with *Spetsnaz* will deny their brutality, which extends even to their own members, because speed of results is paramount. They will kill their own wounded – the group cannot transport a wounded man, nor can it let him fall into the hands of the enemy. And if a rocket launcher or an aircraft carrying nuclear weapons is ready for action, they will attack it even if it means the inevitable destruction of the entire group.

Let us examine one case study which underlines both the importance and effectiveness of operational intelligence. The greatest interest for the staff of military districts is not the political situation or technology but pure military information: the deployment, numbers, equipment and plans of the troops of a probable enemy in sectors where an attack by Soviet forces is likely. An agent who had been recruited by the second department of the intelligence directorate of the Byelorussian Military District on West German territory selected places for parachute landings by the *Spetsnaz* groups. He photographed these locations and made diagrams. Obviously, since the prime motive was sabotage, his choices were near important bridges, dams and narrow passes in lakeland areas. His photographs were transported by courier into East Germany to one of the intelligence points of the Byelorussian Military District. Copies were also sent to the third and fourth departments of the Byelorussian Military District intelligence directorate. While they were being studied, an officer noticed a group of American soldiers who kept on appearing in close-up. The soldiers were doing something at a kind of metal hatchway on the side of the road, and the suggestion was put forward that they were laying a cable for military communications. This was scotched by officers of the fifth department who had been invited for consultations and who said categorically that the Americans would not have a cable in that region. The laying of military cable on West German territory would in any case be discovered by agents of the military district. In the opinion of the signals officers, the photographs showed that the soldiers' work was unlikely to be concerned with cables. The photographs were immediately dispatched to the GRU information service, where a new suggestion was put forward. Could these not be anti-personnel land mines which are prepared in peace-time where Soviet sabotage units might be active in the event of war? This suggestion greatly alarmed the GRU leadership. The fifth directorate immediately gave orders to all intelligence directorates running agents in West Germany to pay particular attention to the activities of small groups of soldiers in the neighbourhood of important bridges, dams, railway stations and crossroads. At the same time, the first GRU directorate gave similar orders to all its residents in West Germany. A month later, the information service of the GRU had at its disposal thousands of photographs of groups of soldiers working at metallic hatchways. Every hatchway that had been discovered was marked on a map. This alone did not permit a final conclusion to be drawn about the significance of the hatchways, and the GRU had a series of enlargements taken from a distance of not more than one metre. The photographic interpreters were interested to see that the thickness of the hatchways was no greater than that of the wall of a good safe, but the locks would have been the envy of any bank. This led to the opinion that the land mines were of a more complicated design. Further analysis showed that the mine-shafts were very deep, and sometimes placed at some hundreds of metres from the object which they were supposed to destroy in case of war. It was this which finally convinced the specialists that it was not a case of ordinary land mines, but of a nuclear variety, whose purpose was not to counter a parachute attack but to halt all Soviet troops in case they began an attack on Europe. Simultaneously, one of the GRU residencies on West German territory acquired documentary evidence confirming the conclusions of the information service.

The possibility of nuclear land mines being used completely disrupted all Soviet plans for a *blitzkrieg* attack on Europe. The general staff, the Ministry of Defence and the Central Committee would now have to find new ways of attack, new methods of employing their troops and ways and means of surmounting strong radioactive fallout caused by the underground explosions. In a word, all tactics, operational methods and strategic plans would have to be changed. All this was thanks to the fact that the new NATO tactics had become known to the general staff in good time.

Chapter Eight

Tactical Reconnaissance

There is yet another level to the practice of military intelligence. Intelligence organs and detachments subject to tactical units and formations of divisional strength and below, which facilitate their military operations, come under the heading of tactical reconnaissance. Their activities are under the full control of operational intelligence, which of course comes under the control of the GRU central apparatus. So all tactical reconnaissance organs have, in exactly the same way as operational intelligence organs, a twofold subordination. The head of reconnaissance of a division is subordinated to the chief of army intelligence, more accurately the first group of the Army Intelligence Department. The chief of regimental reconnaissance is subordinate to the regimental chief of staff and the chief of divisional reconnaissance. Each motorised-rifle and tank division has on its strength an independent reconnaissance battalion. The word 'independent' shows that the battalion does not form part of the regiment but is directly subject to the divisional staff. Each of the four motorised-rifle and tank regiments on the strength of a division has a reconnaissance company. Reconnaissance companies are controlled by the regimental reconnaissance chiefs. Artillery and anti-aircraft missile regiments are not included as their reconnaissance detachments are not active in the enemy's rear.

A divisional independent reconnaissance battalion consists of a headquarters, a deep reconnaissance company, two reconnaissance companies, a company electronic reconnaissance and auxiliary services.

Deep Reconnaissance
The deep reconnaissance company is the smallest but the best of all the companies and batteries of the division. There are

twenty-seven men in the company including six officers and an ensign. It has a small headquarters of the commander and a sergeant-major, and five reconnaissance groups of four men, each with an officer at its head. There is a total of six jeeps, each group having one and one for the commander.

The company's task is to discover and destroy enemy rocket launchers in its divisional sector. Deep reconnaissance groups are deployed in the enemy's rear by helicopter, either with or without their jeeps, to depths of from thirty to 100 kilometres.

On discovering an enemy rocket installation, the group immediately reports it to the staff. Should the rocket be ready for launching, the group must attack it. However, unlike the *Spetsnaz* groups, the group will not kill its wounded unless the action is on foot – a rare occurrence. The deep reconnaissance company may also be called upon to kidnap staff officers and to hunt for their staffs, but only in cases where the commander of a division is certain that there are no enemy nuclear facilities in his divisional sector.

The Reconnaissance Companies of the Battalion have exactly similar organisation. In each company there are three tanks, seven reconnaissance vehicles and ten motorcycles.

The Electronic Reconnaissance Companies have eighty men and thirty vehicles with electronic equipment. The company operates only from its own territory. Among its tasks are intercepting and deciphering radio conversations of the enemy, taking bearings on radio stations and radio locators, and monitoring the extent to which its own side observes radio security regulations.

Each motor-rifle and tank regiment has its own reconnaissance company. Regimental companies operate at a depth of up to fifty kilometres as against the battalion company's operation to eighty kilometres. All these companies penetrate enemy territory under their own power, using gaps in the enemy's defence. The basic method of obtaining information is the capture and cruel interrogation of prisoners.

The Soviet army has approximately 180 motor-rifle and tank divisions. Many of these, especially those deployed in the rear, are under strength. Undermanning is never allowed, however, in the case of reconnaissance detachments. There is about the same number of independent reconnaissance battalions, and there are also about 700 regimental reconnaissance companies. In other words there are about 95,000 men directly under GRU command in tactical reconnaissance. We have not included in this number the strength of chemical, engineering and artillery reconnaissance companies independent of these.

Chapter Nine

The Training and Privileges of Personnel

These are the educational institutions which take part in the training of personnel for Soviet military intelligence: the Intelligence Faculty at the General Staff Academy; the Training Centre of Illegals; the Military-Diplomatic Academy; the Reconnaissance Faculty of the Frunze Military Academy; the Reconnaissance Faculty of the Naval Academy; the Special Faculty of the Military Signals Academy; the Military Institute of Foreign Languages; the Cherepovetski Higher Military Engineering School for Communications; the Special Faculty of the Higher Military Naval School of Radio Electronics; the *Spetsnaz* Faculty of the Ryazan Higher Parachute School; the Reconnaissance Faculty of the Kiev Higher Military Command School; and the Special Faculty of the Second Kharkov Higher Military Aviation and Engineering School.

This list gives an impression of the extent of the training of specialists for the GRU system. Some of these educational establishments are devoted exclusively to this work, others have only one faculty. However, in any case, we are talking of many thousands of first-class specialists who go into military intelligence every year. All the higher military schools give instruction at university level to their students. The best of these subsequently enter the academies which provide a second university education.

Students entering the Soviet Army's higher military training establishments undergo a period of instruction which lasts for four to five years. The minimum age is seventeen, maximum twenty-four. Candidates must have finished secondary education and be of normal mental and physical development with a suitable ideological background. They sit an entrance examination and are interviewed by a medical commission; they then take a competitive examination. The vast majority of them have no idea of the true character of the educational establishment they have chosen. In some cases, the name of the school gives a reasonably exact idea of the subjects studied in it. The Ulyanov Guards Higher Tank Command School leaves little to the imagination. But what does a name like the Serpukhovski Higher Command Engineering School tell us? If a candidate chooses it, he may be surprised to find himself learning about strategic missile troops. Signals schools are largely the same – the candidate has little idea of exactly what subjects are studied there. He selects one of them, the Cherepovetski school, say, and finds himself in strategic intelligence. The point is that there is no choice.

Graduates of higher command schools receive the rank of lieutenant and a university diploma on graduating. Graduates of higher military engineering schools receive the rank of engineer lieutenant and an engineering diploma. After graduation, the officer is posted to a unit on the instructions of the General Staff, and from the first day of his service his fight with his fellow officers for the right of entry to the academy begins. The academy is *the* passport to the higher echelons of the Army. Without passing through the academy, the officer may serve on until major or lieutenant-colonel level at the most. Success in the academy opens wide horizons and speeds up progress on the promotion ladder. The officer may submit his first application to the academy after three years of service. The application is confirmed at every level of command, beginning with his immediate superior. Any higher commander may hold up the application under any pretext: that the officer is too young; too old; too stupid; or too clever. In which case the officer will put off his application until the next year ... and the next year, and so on possibly for all his twenty-five years of service.

There are more than fifteen military academies in the Soviet Army, but for most officers it does not matter which one he gets into. The important thing is to get into one of them. If his commanders decide that an officer is suitable, he must still pass examinations and undergo a rigorous entrance competition. The period of study at all the academies is three years, and they are all similar bar one, the General Staff Academy. To enter it there is no competition and no examinations, nor are there applications for entry. Candidates are selected by the Central Committee from the number of the most successful and dedicated colonels and generals up to and including colonel-general, who have already completed their study at one of the military academies.

The General Staff Academy is the passport to the very highest levels of Soviet military leadership. The colonel or general continues to serve and never suspects that he may suddenly receive from the Central Committee an invitation to attend yet a third spell of university education. The General Staff Academy is the highest dream of the most eager careerists.

Let us examine the progress of an intelligence officer on the promotion ladder. As a graduate of the intelligence faculty of the Kiev Higher Command School, for example, he will be posted to the command of a reconnaissance detachment of a regiment or division. Here begins the officer's gradual upward movement on the service ladder, from platoon commander to company commander to commander of regimental reconnaissance and deputy commander of reconnaissance battalions. To secure further promotion, the officer must now enter the reconnaissance faculty of the Frunze military academy. This same faculty is also open to graduates of the *Spetsnaz* faculty of the Ryazan Higher Parachute School. All officers study there together and then return to their own units, only this time with a higher command.

So far all this is straightforward, provided that the officer's superiors co-operate in signing the necessary documents. But one institute, the Military Institute instructing in foreign languages, is rather peculiar. This is a privileged establishment for the children of the highest echelons of the Soviet Army. The Institute exists on the same basis as the Military Academy, although young people enter it according to the rules laid down for military schools. This means, in fact, that a candidate's father has only to worry about placing his little son on the first rung of the military ladder and the ladder itself will move upwards.

The period of study in the institute is from five to seven years depending on the faculty. The student receives education to the level of that of the military school and the rank of lieutenant; he then proceeds with his training as he would in a normal military academy. That is to say, these scions of the military aristocracy are spared the rigours of genuine military service as well as the cruel competition between officers for the right of entry to a military academy. Everything proceeds automatically.

The Institute is not only a stepping-stone to the highest Army ranks, but to the highest ranks of the KGB too. The conditions of acceptance are naturally graded according to rank: for the children of colonel-generals and higher, there are no examinations; the children of lieutenant-generals undergo a very cursory examination; and the children of major-generals undergo the most rigorous examination. However, in order to soften this clear class distinction, the Institute every year accepts a ten per cent intake of 'non-aristocrats', sons of colonels and majors, sometimes even of workers and *kolkhozniks*.

Discipline and competition are fearsome. Should any student commit the slightest offence, he is speedily expelled from the Institute in disgrace. But there is a deeply-entrenched set of privileges too. For the sons of lieutenant-generals, and colonel-generals even more so, the special entrance provides for the appointment of individual tutors and the taking of examinations privately at home, so that the candidate does not get nervous. For colonel-generals and above, there exists the privilege of being able to send not only their sons to the Institute, but also their daughters, who constitute a special little group. The girls are given instruction in French for the sake of prestige and in English for obvious commercial reasons. They, together with everybody else, receive officer's rank. They will find their way into the Ministry of Defence.

After the Institute's final examinations, interested organisations carry out their selection of the graduates. The first selection is carried out by the KGB and the GRU according to the principle of 'one for you, one for me'. There is no friction, firstly because the system has been laid down for many years and secondly because KGB and GRU have different interests.

The KGB is quite happy to choose the sons of high-ranking, serving KGB officers, but the GRU devotes its attentions largely to the proletarian ten per cent. For two principal reasons the GRU has had a long-standing rule that it will not admit the sons of high-placed parents into its organisation, nor will it admit children of GRU officers whatever post they occupy. Only after a father retires from the GRU can his son be considered for admission. The reasoning goes that if a son is refused something the father may refuse the same thing to all his subordinates. Secondly, there is no father who really wants to risk his own career by linking it with that of a son who is on agent work and to whom anything could happen. This principle of the GRU's has to a very great extent eradicated corruption in the selection of officers, although corruption flourishes in other GRU fields of activity. (The KGB has adopted diametrically opposed principles. Everywhere within it are the children of Tchekists, frequently under the direct supervision of their fathers. This is justified by the false notion of handing down traditions from father to son.)

*

The unclassified name of the institution is 'military unit 35576'. Its secret designation is the Soviet Army Academy. Its top secret designation is the Military-Diplomatic Academy of the Soviet Army. Regardless of the abundance of names, none gives any idea of what is studied there. If somebody wanted to convey an idea of its activities by means of a name, then that name would most probably be something like the Military Academy of Agent Intelligence. Very few people inside the Soviet Union know of the existence of this academy, and should any officer ever hear a rumour about it, and write an application to enter it, immediate enquiries would be made to establish the source of the information. One may rest assured that a culprit would be found and put in prison for spreading government secrets. For spreading a secret like the existence of the Soviet Army Academy the sentence is ten years in prison, perhaps fifteen, perhaps even the 'ultimate sanction'. Those connected with the Academy understand this rule and obey it enthusiastically.

The GRU seeks out candidates for the Academy and secretly suggests to officers that they should enter. Before making this proposal to an officer, the officer will of course have been very carefully checked out by the GRU, who must not only be certain that he will agree but will also have obliged him to sign a document about the divulging of military secrets. In this document are described all the unpleasant things which await him, should he decide to share his secrets with anybody else. However, they do not tell him any secrets. They simply tell him that there exists a certain academy which is keen to welcome him as a student. To his question as to what sort of studies he will undergo, he receives the answer that the work is very interesting. There will be no soldiers and no hierarchy of rank, and the conditions of life are vastly better than those of any other organisation known to him.

At the outset this is all they will entrust to him. The GRU holds nobody against his will and is perfectly frank about future privileges. For the GRU officer who completes the Academy, success is assured – unless he makes a mistake, in which case retribution is equally swift. He may either be deprived of overseas work and be sent instead to work in the central organs of the GRU in Moscow; he may be deprived of work in the GRU and sent back to the Army; and finally, he may be shot. All of these punishments, not only the last, are regarded as harsh in the extreme. The first means the end of overseas life, and GRU officers are envious even of dustmen overseas. The second means an end to privilege and the sweet life within the GRU, and a return to the grindstone of life as an ordinary Soviet officer. The third is only marginally worse.

The Soviet Army Academy is located in Moscow on Narodnogo Opolchenia Street, but many of its secret branches are scattered all over the place disguised as innocent offices, flats or hotels. The central building reminds one of an elegant museum with its Greek colonnade and richly carved ornamentation. Around it are several large buildings, and the whole is surrounded by a very high iron lattice-work fence. The area wallows in greenery so that nothing can be seen. There are no name plates or number plates on the building. From the outside there is little to indicate that it is secret. Only sometimes on the upper storeys and in certain windows can one see grilles and casements covered in cord nets, an indication that within those rooms there is work on top secret documents being carried out. The string nets are so that no pieces of paper can be blown out of the windows by draughts.

The Academy is an integral part of the GRU. The chief of the Academy has the military rank of colonel-general and is a deputy head of the GRU, not of course first deputy head. The chief of the Academy has four deputies who are lieutenant-generals beneath him. These are the first deputy and the deputies for the political, administrative-technical and academic sections.

The first deputy is in charge of the graduate school, four faculties and academic courses. The political deputy is responsible for the state of political awareness and the morale of all officers of the Academy. The administrative-technical deputy is responsible for the personnel department and the security department (with the commandant's office and a company of security guards) together with the finance, stores and transport departments. Under him there are also the libraries, including collections of secret and top secret literature. The deputy for the academic section has under him the academic sub-faculties which are headed by major-generals. These sub-faculties are strategic agent intelligence, operational agent intelligence and *Spetsnaz* (dealing with the armed forces of likely enemies), strategic and operational trade-craft of the Soviet Army, foreign languages and study of countries, history of international relations and diplomatic practice and, finally, Marxist-Leninist philosophy.

The first and second faculties prepare their students for the central GRU apparatus. However, the first faculty is called the Special Services Faculty and the second the Military-Diplomatic Faculty, and it is officially considered that the first faculty prepares officers for civilian cover – embassies, civil airlines, merchant navy, trade representations – while the second faculty prepares its students for military cover. But we must again remember that Soviet military attachés are the same GRU officers as those who work under civil cover. They face the same tasks and use the same methods as all other officers of the GRU. For this reason the instructional programme in both faculties is absolutely identical. Furthermore, when students have completed their studies, in whichever of the two faculties that might be, the GRU will post them under whatever cover they consider suitable. Many of the officers who have studied in the first faculty will find themselves working in military organisations and vice-versa. The artificial distinction exists in order to further the following aims: to confuse Western intelligence services and to create the illusion that there is some difference between military attachés and other GRU officers; to segregate the students for security reasons (a defector will not know all his fellow students, only half – with this in mind the first faculty is isolated from the central block of the academy buildings); to simplify control over individual students; and finally, since the academy is after all designated as a military-diplomatic academy, it seems wise that not all its faculties should bear names connected with espionage.

The third faculty deals with operational agent intelligence and

Spetsnaz intelligence, preparing officers for intelligence directorates of military districts. There exists a deep enmity between officers of the first two faculties and officers of the third. An officer of one of the two strategic faculties, however newly arrived, feels the very deepest contempt for all those studying in the third faculty. He will be going abroad but the despised third faculty student will recruit agents from Soviet or satellite territory only. But fate can be cruel – and kind. When the worst (usually the most arrogant) officers have graduated from the strategic faculties, they are sent to operational agent intelligence; in their place are taken the best of the officers graduating from the third faculty.

The fourth faculty, like the first, is not located on the academy premises. Moreover, its individual courses and groups are separated among themselves in conditions of the strictest secrecy. The fourth faculty trains foreigners – Poles, Germans, Czechs, Hungarians, Bulgars, Mongols and Cubans. Naturally, not one of these has ever set foot in the academy buildings and has no idea where the academy is located; equally naturally, the Soviet trainees in the academy must not have even the slightest contact with their 'brothers'.

For each of these students in the Soviet Army academy, a special personal cover story will have been worked out. Frequently, many of them will study for a year in some normal military academy concerned with tank or artillery studies, for example, before spending their three to four years on secret premises. And these students do not receive diplomas from the Soviet Army Academy. Their diplomas come from, for example, the Tank Warfare Academy. Only a handful of people will know what is hidden under this name.

The academic courses are something different. These are designed not to provide a complete training, but only partial one, and the period of study is only one year. They are attended principally by the most experienced officers and those with the greatest future prospects, who were chosen for entry to strategic faculties of the academy but then transferred by the GRU into the diplomatic (civil) or overseas trade academy where they completed a full course of study. They are considered on a par with the other civil students and carry out their specialised training in their spare time and receive the same diplomas as the graduates of the two strategic faculties, having already received genuine diplomatic diplomas. This is the most secret part of Soviet intelligence after illegals, for even genuine 'clean' diplomats consider them their own kind and do not suspect their intelligence connections. The academic courses are also attended by graduates of the Military Foreign Languages Institute who have been chosen by the GRU for work abroad. The GRU uses them in residencies mainly for duties with technical and technical-operational services. After a first assignment abroad these may, provided they have served successfully, enter the academy in one of the strategic faculties. Lastly, the academy receives specialists from other fields whom the GRU invites to work in technical services or on information work.

There is a post-graduate school too, which prepares scientific personnel for the GRU and also instructors for the academy itself. An officer who has completed one of the strategic faculties, and has been abroad on agent work and shown good results, is accepted by the post-graduate school for a period of instruction of two to three years during which he must prepare and defend a scientific dissertation on a subject chosen by himself. The resulting qualification is a scientific degree, Master of Military Science.

Who is eligible? This is a very complex problem. The candidate who hopes to please the GRU must fulfil the following conditions: racial purity – there must be no Jewish blood as far back as the fourth generation (the KGB has no such restriction); ideological stability and purity; membership of the communist party; the absence of any contact with overseas, excepting the 'liberation' of Hungary and Czechoslovakia and the 'defence of socialism in eastern Europe'. He must have a wife and children of complete ideological and racial purity. He must have strong and reliable family connections, on his own side and his wife's. There must be no compromising material on the files of any of their relatives. None of his relatives may have been either prisoners of war in Germany, nor on Soviet territory under the temporary occupation of German forces. And there must be no signs whatsoever of alcoholism, sexual promiscuity, family problems, corruption and so on, nor must the officer have any prominent distinguishing features or speech defects.

One of the most difficult things in selecting candidates is to find people who understand the political situation in the world and can clearly see possible future developments without being secret free-thinkers. Obviously anyone who is politically inept is not acceptable to the GRU, but if a man is moderately intelligent, there is always the danger that secret doubts will begin to penetrate his head. Naturally, when this rare creature is found he is instantly made to sit meaningless examinations and, from the very first day, accorded appropriate honours.

In a classless society, everybody is equal and life is therefore happy and free. All people are friends and brothers and nobody will try to do his neighbour down. People may pursue their ambitions without let or hindrance. Of course, if you live in the country, you cannot move to the city, still less the capital Moscow, without the permission of the Central Committee. Society may be classless, all right, but it is divided, for the good of the people, into parts – you have the right to live in the city or you have not. You may rightly say that you would prefer to live in the city, but you are branded from birth – if you were born in the country, you must stay there and so must your children and grandchildren – for their own good. Unless – unless you do something like become a GRU officer. Immediately, you will find yourself in Moscow, with a permanent residence permit. This is good news for not only you, but your children and grandchildren and great-grandchildren and great-great-grandchildren down to the fortieth generation, who will all have Moscow residence permits and will legally reside in Moscow.

It is as if you had moved onto a higher sphere, as if you and your relations had suddenly been ennobled. You should draw your family tree on the wall of your apartment so that future generations of your family will know who it was who lifted them up to the heights.

In capitalist societies, where everybody is naturally out for each other's blood, people move around chaotically, causing untold social problems. These could all be eradicated with the introduction of residence permits on the Soviet model. The Moscow residence permit, logically, is the first privilege of a GRU officer. There are others, of course. For example, an ordinary general staff officer is unable to buy a car during the whole of his life unless of course he steals or is sent abroad. A GRU officer may in three years buy not only a car, but also an apartment. Drawing another distinction, it is often asked how much more a GRU officer abroad earns in comparison with the same officer in Moscow. It is impossible to answer this question sensibly, because in Moscow the officer spends money which is to all practical purposes incapable of buying anything except food of rather inferior quality and equally inferior clothes. He who is sent abroad, however, receives foreign currency and can buy everything he needs both while he is abroad and at home in the Soviet Union in the special foreign currency shops. In possessing foreign currency a GRU officer becomes a man of completely different class, very sharply distinguished from all those who do not have it. Special shops and restaurants are open to him, where he can buy anything he wants, without queueing. The ordinary Soviet citizen, including the general staff officer or even the GRU officer who does not serve abroad, may not even enter these shops.

So Soviet society is as racial as it can possibly be, only race is not determined by the colour of your skin but by whether you have the right to travel abroad or not. Imagine any country, France perhaps, putting up outside shops the announcement that: 'Nobody of French nationality is allowed to enter this shop. Only those on the list of the Central Committee of the Communist Party are admitted.' But in the Soviet Union there are everywhere shops, hotels, restaurants which Russians may not enter, because they are Russian. Life for a GRU officer possessing foreign currency is on an infinitely wider scale than for the 270 million who are deprived of the right to hold foreign currency. And once he has become a representative of the upper class, he becomes inordinately jealous of his right, fearing above anything the loss of the privilege which allows him to travel abroad. This is why he defends himself against any revelation about his own person, against any, even the most insignificant, contacts with the police. This is why he tries to hide from his superiors even the smallest shortcomings. This is why he is capable of any dirty trick upon anybody, including his own comrades, when what is at stake is whether he should remain another year in a hot, humid, subtropical posting – or return early to Moscow.

Conclusion

For a GRU officer, there are countries in which he dreams of working. There are also countries in which he would rather not work. There are cities he dreams of, and cities he sees in nightmares.

The dream city for a GRU officer is Peking. Its infernal counterpart—Tokyo. This might appear strange, because for the top brass of the GRU quite the reverse is true: Tokyo is heaven, Peking hell. But the interests of a GRU officer are directly opposed to the interests of the top brass. The top brass desire high productivity, while the work force has rather different aims.

Imagine that you are lucky and are posted to China. What awaits you? A vast, splendid embassy behind high walls. Chit-chat with colleagues from other embassies, gossip about the state of health of the Chinese leaders and the Ambassador's wife. After five years your return home, obviously without having recruited any agents. But nobody will bawl you out for it, you will not have your epaulettes torn off, no one will call you lazy or a coward. Everyone understands that you have been in hell, where serious work is impossible. . . .

And now imagine that you are an unlucky spy and the GRU post you to Tokyo. Both you and the GRU top brass know that there are no laws against spying there, that conditions for spying are ideal. So what awaits you? Exhausting stressful work, fifteen to seventeen hours a day, with no rest days and no feast days. No matter how many secrets you manage to acquire it will never be enough. No matter how many agents you recruit it will never be enough. Your paradise will be snowed under with cipher cables from Moscow addressed to the resident saying: 'You have seventy operational officers! Where's your productivity? What you managed to get yesterday we have already received from Hong

Kong! From Berlin! From illegals! Where are the secrets!!!???' You may rest assured that this question is put by the GRU daily to the resident—who will in turn ask you the same question, pounding the table with his enormous fist. He will fight for the kind of productivity that can only be achieved through merciless competition. If your output is not up to scratch you will simply be sent home and your career broken.

Personally I have never been to Tokyo, but I have had to work in a country which was considered 'paradise' by the GRU top brass. Understandably, for us it was 'hell'. A weak police system in that country meant that the other residents continually used it as an intermediate base for their operations, and it was a busy crossing point for GRU illegals, too. All of them had to be taken care of and helped. Acting as a supply base for agent network operations is rather like serving in a signals unit during a war: as long as communication lines are maintained nobody remembers you, but should communications be interrupted the signaller is sent to a penal battalion forthwith, charged with the failure of the entire operation. The difference between us and the signals boys lay in the fact that no matter how well we maintained supplies, how successful our own work was, we also had to recruit agents. After all, we were living in 'paradise', where the police was weak and Soviet diplomats were never expelled.

I'd like to beg all who are responsible for the security of the West: be human. Do expel Soviet spies occasionally. By expelling one you enable others to reduce their frantic activity. A spy is a human being. He bears on his shoulders the immense pressure of the gigantic GRU establishment, and he has no excuse for any lapses. He needs one, so be human.

Who should be expelled first? The answer is obvious: the resident. The expulsion of the resident is equivalent to clearing the King off the chess-board: it spells checkmate to the 'residentura', no matter how aggressive and successful it is. Usually the local police know who he is. He is easy to identify. He has already served abroad for twelve to fifteen years, he has been very active and, judging by the signs, successful. Now here he is serving abroad again, in a senior diplomatic post, and hardly ever leaving the embassy, but sitting there motionless, like a spider. Clearly it is against him that all forces must be mobilised. This is not easy. He breaks no laws, does not speed up and down the motorways day and night, carries no stolen secrets in his car. But he is more dangerous than all his officers put together.

There is a deep-seated and erroneous belief that known residents should not be allowed into the country. Sometimes they aren't, sometimes they are simply not granted entry visas. This is a mistake. I will try to explain, using my own resident as an example. He was a man of unflinching will and powerful intellect, a true ace of spies: careful, perfidious, calculating and fearless. He was promoted to major-general at the age of thirty-six, and he had a brilliant career in front of him in the upper echelons of the GRU. But all he wanted was to be a resident, and as a result he remained a major-general. Without any doubt the Security Services in the West knew him well. Prior to one of his postings abroad the Soviet Ministry of Foreign Affairs asked for a Belgian visa for him. It was refused. They asked for a French one – again refused. Then a West German one – refused again. Finally a small country with a soft, friendly government agreed to grant him entry. The GRU gave the resident his final briefing, which of course included the names and addresses of the members of the network run by the 'residentura'. As soon as he arrived in the country he started extending the network speedily and vigorously, until it was working successfully against the USA, against Belgium, against France, against all the countries which had refused him entry. In other words, barring a resident from a country does not mean rendering his network ineffective (see Appendix C).

Now imagine another set of circumstances. Supposing the first country approached, in this case Belgium, had issued the visa. The resident would be briefed, let into all the 'residentura' secrets, and would arrive in the country. However if, three to four months later, Belgium found some reason or other to expel him, the results of this would be threefold:

1. The resident will have had time to disrupt the existing system of work in the residency but not to build up a new system.

2. Having to leave the country suddenly, the resident will leave his army without a commanding officer. Time will be needed for the successor's visa application and more time to brief the new resident. In the interim the residency will remain inactive.

3. The experienced resident, on returning to Moscow, will be completely neutralised. For the following three to four years, visa applications cannot be sent for him either to France or West

Germany or any other country that Belgium will have notified as an ally.

One experienced, authoritative, demanding and merciless resident serving in a neutral country with ten officers under his command can sometimes harm the West more than two hundred very active GRU officers working in the USA, Great Britain, West Germany or France. This is not only a matter of my opinion, it is also the opinion held by Moscow Centre, and it was the opinion held by my first resident, who taught me unforgettable lessons in concentration on target, persistence and mad risk. I am sincerely sorry that he has stayed the other side of the barricade....

How should one go about the business of expulsion? The short answer is: as noisily as possible. To expel a Soviet spy is of course a victory. But to expel him noisily means that you are making as much capital out of the victory as you can. The silent expulsion of a Soviet spy is an action directed against one man. The noisy expulsion is a slap in the face for the GRU, for the KGB; it is an action directed against all their spies, against thousands of unstable people prepared to listen to the proposals of the Soviet intelligence service. Here is another example encountered during my work.

I had a reasonably good relationship with a young man who agreed to 'lose' his passport. In return he agreed to 'find' some money. This was the first step towards the morass. Further well-tried steps were planned which would have pushed him deeper in each time; once in, he would never have been able to get out. However, on the day scheduled for a meeting, an insignificant local paper published an item stating that fifty per cent of the Soviet Embassy staff were spies. So at our meeting, instead of losing the money I had with me and finding his passport, I had to spend the time proving to him that the news item was a lie. And it really was a barefaced lie, as at that time not fifty but eighty per cent of the Embassy staff were spies. I managed to convince the young man. We remained good friends ... but nothing more. He did not take the crucial step. Should you, young man, be reading my book, my greetings to you. I am glad for your sake, in spite of the fact that at the time I felt my failure deeply. But what can a poor GRU spy do in a situation when the powerful free Western press publishes such items at the least suitable moment?

Finally the question arises as to how many Soviet spies should

172

be expelled. The only answer is: *all*. What do you need them for? Why keep them in your country? They are professionals specially selected and trained to destroy your country. If you have the evidence to prove that they are spies – expel them. Sometimes the theory is put forward that it is better to unearth a spy and keep him under surveillance than to expel him, as then a new one will be sent in and we will not know whom to keep under surveillance. That is correct. But every expelled spy represents a nightmare to the new ones, who fear deeply being appointed as replacements. Secondly, intelligence experience is much more valuable than any amount of education, and one experienced spy is a hundred times more dangerous than a young, green one. The more inexperienced spies you have in your country the more mistakes will be made, the easier it will be to watch them.

But if we expel people, runs the argument, the Soviet Union will retaliate and expel our innocent diplomats from Moscow. That is so. But to that there is an antidote – you must expel large groups of diplomats simultaneously. Look at these statistics: Holland expelled one – the Soviet Union's reply : two. Turkey expelled one – the reply : two. But if you increase the number to five the Soviet reply will be five or fewer. Canada expelled thirteen – the reply : two. France expelled forty-seven – the reply : nil.

Great Britain simultaneously expelled 105 (the entire staff of the GRU and KGB residencies). There was no comeback. If you take similar action against Soviet spies I guarantee that your diplomats in Moscow will be safe. I guarantee that your diplomats will be greatly respected, and that the Soviet leadership will look for opportunities to improve its relations with you. The Soviet leadership understands and acknowledges strength. But only strength and nothing else. The Soviet Union can respect the sovereignty of any country, no matter how small it looks on the map. But the Soviet Union respects the sovereignty only of those nations who respect their own sovereignty and defend it.

For GRU Officers Only

I was condemned to death by the Military College of the Supreme Court according to article 64a. My crime – betrayal of the homeland. I still plead not guilty as charged. The betrayers of the homeland are those who are now in the Kremlin. The betrayers of the homeland are those who shot millions of the best Russian farmers. Russia has always grown wheat. Grain was its most important export. Those who have made of Russia an importer of grain – they are the betrayers who should be sentenced under article 64. On the eve of war the communist leaders shot the best marshals and generals. They were motivated not by the interests of the homeland, but by the desire to hold on to their power. They should be tried in a court of law. For the deaths of the marshals and generals, my people paid the price of tens of millions of lives. Those who are guilty of that should be tried. Those in the Kremlin who have brought my people to complete moral and physical degradation – they are the traitors. These people are driving my comrades to their deaths in Afghanistan, demanding the deaths of innocent people – they are the criminals.

If they at some future time should be judged and given their just deserts, and if, then, my country then considered me to be a traitor also for deserting it, then I am ready to take my punishment, but only after they have taken theirs.

When I was in the GRU I could see two ways to protest: either I could commit suicide; or I could escape to the West, explain my disagreement with the communists and then commit suicide. I chose the second way, which is not a whit easier than than the first. It is an agonising way. If any GRU officer now finds himself in the same dilemma – to go or to stay – I advise him to think over his decision a hundred times, and then again. If he is thinking of fleeing to the West, then my advice to him is – don't do it. Article

64 will be waiting for him, as will the shameful epithet 'traitor', and an agonising death, maybe even on the frontier itself. My advice would always be – don't go. He shouldn't go until such time as he is certain why he is going. If you want an easy life – don't go. If you like long, luxurious motorcars – don't go, it is not worth it for the sake of a car. If you are attracted to Western women – don't go, theirs are really no better than ours. If you think that in the West it is good, and at home in Russia bad, then you are mistaken – ours is a beautiful country. Don't go for the sake of foreign beauties and wonders.

Only if you know there is no other way for you, if you consider your leaders as criminals, if you yourself do not wish to be a criminal – then you should go. If you are prepared to risk your life for one minute of freedom – then go. If you don't feel yourself a traitor by going – go. If, by going, you can bring nearer the moment when the communists are judged by the people of our country, if you can help your people, if you are then ready to stand before the people and await their decision on your fate – then you must go. You will dream of Mother Russia every night, but go for the sake of her future and I promise you that you will be happy.

Appendix A

Leaders of Soviet Military Intelligence

I soon realised that a history of the GRU would be a very fraught undertaking. It is clear that the very shortest history of the GRU would fill several massive tomes and could only be written after the fall of communist power. The history written in this book consists only of isolated details, only vague outlines of a continent shrouded in the mists. The picture may be made clearer by studying the destiny of those individuals who have held the highest power in Soviet military intelligence. In their destinies the whole history of the organisation is reflected.

ARALOV, Simon Ivanovich: 18.12.1880 - 22.5.1969.
He was born in Moscow to rich merchant parents and educated to follow his father's profession. In 1905 he joined the Tsar's army and served in WWI as a major in military intelligence. A participant in the October Revolution he was one of the creators of the Tcheka. In January 1918 he became chief of the Operational Department of the Moscow military district. Rapidly promoted, in October 1918 he became the first chief of military intelligence until July 1920. In 1920 he moved down to chief of intelligence, 12th Army, and then regained ground commanding intelligence of the S.W. front. After 1921 he was a deputy of the chief of military intelligence, working in Turkey, Latvia and Lithuania as undercover ambassador and later was responsible for setting up residencies in the United States, Germany and Japan. In 1937, dismissed from all posts, he was employed as a deputy director of the Literature Museum. Arrested in 1938, he spent three years under interrogation. In 1941 he was serving as a private in a penal battalion. Four years later, he was a colonel, and when the war was over he was taken back into the GRU. Then, arrested in 1946, he spent ten years in a concentration camp. On his liberation he was immediately appointed deputy to the chief of the GRU. In 1957 he was again dismissed in the Zhukov/ Shtemyenko purge, but lived quietly until his death.

STIGGA, Oskar Ansovich: 1894 - 29.7.38.
Born in Latvia, he served in WWI and became a communist after the Revolution, and a leader of the Red Latvian Riflemen. He engaged in suppressing counter-revolutionaries in Moscow and became a private bodyguard of Lenin. In October 1918 he was a deputy of the chief of military intelligence and immediately moved as an illegal into Poland, Lithuania and Latvia. In 1919 he became chief of intelligence of the Western front, and in August 1920 became chief of military intelligence. Reduced to deputy status after 1922, he travelled extensively as an illegal to create new networks until his recall to Moscow in 1938, when he was shot.

NIKONOV, A.M. (Nikonson): ? - 29.7.38.
It remains uncertain whether this was his real name or simply a party pseudo-myn like Lenin, Stalin, Trotski, Zinoviev and others. His date of birth is unknown. He was chief of military intelligence after Stigga, but it is not known whether Berzin took over from him or from another, so far unidentified, chief of military intelligence. He too was executed in the great terror of 1938.

2nd Grade Army Commissar BERZIN, Yan Karlovich (real name Kyuzis Peteris): 13.11.1889 - 29.7.38.
Born in Latvia, Berzin joined the Social-Democratic Party in 1904. He was conscripted into the army in the First World War but deserted and went underground. He took part in the October Revolution and afterwards he worked in the central apparatus of the NKVD and in the NKVD in Latvia. One of the main organisers of the 'Red Terror', he initiated the hostages system. He was also a fervent supporter of the establishment of a communist dictatorship in Latvia and one of the organisers and leaders of the Latvian Red Army (subsequently the 15th Army). He was head of a special department of this army and played a part in the suppression of the Russian sailors' mutiny at Kronstadt. He particularly distinguished himself in the course of the pursuit and liquidation of captured sailors. From April 1921 he was Deputy Head of Intelligence Directorate (GRU) but, from his first days in military intelligence, he was, *de facto*, its head. With effect from March 1924 he became its head legally as well. He was one of the most talented, industrious and successful heads of intelligence, the creator of the most powerful and successful intelligence organisations in existence anywhere. He personally recruited and ran the most outstanding intelligence officers – Yakov Mrachkovski (Gorev), Moshe Milstein (Mikhail M), Ruth and Rolf Werner, Richard Sorge, Lev Manevich, Sandor Rado, Karl Ramm, Aino Kuusinen, Ignati Reis and the most eminent intelligence officer of the 20th century, Konstantin Efremov. In 1936 Berzin transferred the Soviet military intelligence command post from Moscow to Madrid, where he carried out his most notable recruitments while he was working under cover, officially designated as chief military adviser to the Republican Government. In order to sustain this cover story his deputies Uritski and Unshlikht carried out his duties in Moscow. On returning from Spain he continued to lead military intelligence. On 13 May 1938 he was arrested and on 29 July he was shot.

UNSHLIKHT, Iosif Stanislavovich: 19.12.1879 - 29.7.1938.
An hereditary Polish nobleman and an active member of the Polish (left-wing) Social-Democratic Party, he was one of the leaders of the October Revolution. Immediately after the revolution he became a member of the NKVD college. He began the policy of state terror before Dzerzhinsky, and at one time he was considered by Soviet historians as the 'first founder of the Tcheka' at the same time as Dzerzhinsky was considered the 'chief founder of the Tcheka'. A fervent supporter of the establishment of communism in Poland, in 1920 he was a member of the 'Polish Revolutionary Government'. From 1921–23 he was deputy chairman of the All-Russian Tcheka and one of the fathers of the 'Red Terror'. From 1923 he was deputy head of the registration directorate (GRU). In the interests of cover he constantly filled responsible posts in the Soviet Government and the Red Army. He travelled abroad several times with false documents to organise illegal work in Poland, Lithuania and Germany. In 1935–36 during Berzin's absence he carried out the duties of chief of the GRU

177

although he remained in fact only deputy to Berzin. He was shot with Berzin in the cellar of the 'Hotel Metropole' in Moscow.

Corps Commander URITSKI, Solomon Petrovich: 1895–1937 was chief of the GRU during Berzin's absence. He was shot in the first wave of the Terror.

Commissar-General of State Security EZHOV, Nikolai Ivanovich: 1895–1940.
A petty official who only joined the Bolsheviks when it became clear that they had won, he occupied insignificant party posts in the provinces, but from 1927 Ezhov was in Stalin's personal secretariat. In 1930 he was in charge of the Central Committee Personnel Department and in 1935 Party Secretary, controller of NKVD work. In 1936 he became Peoples' Commissar for Internal Affairs and Commissar-General for State Security. In 1937–38 there began under his leadership the 'great purge' which started as a purge of the NKVD and was then extended to the army, the party and the entire country. On 29 July 1938 there was a repeat purge of the GRU and, having liquidated the whole of the leadership and the operational staff, he took over its control, thus establishing a monopoly of secret activities in the state. From this moment on it would be impossible for the activites of the GRU and NKVD to be subject to reciprocal checking. However, the monopoly alarmed Stalin and 29 July saw the beginning of Ezhov's downfall. In October he was removed from his post. He was arrested in January 1939 and liquidated after atrocious torture. According to unconfirmed data, he was buried alive at the NKVD sanatorium at Sukhanovo.

One of the bloodiest careers in the history of mankind. Ezhov was the shortest serving Chief of the GRU and suffered the most painful death. The date of his death has not been established with certainty; there are grounds for thinking it could have been on 4 June 1940. There are also grounds for believing that Ivan Serov, a future chief of the GRU, played a personal part in Ezhov's death.

Lieut-General of Aviation PROSKUROV, Ivan Iosifovich: ? - 5.7.1940.
An outstanding Soviet intelligence officer and fighter pilot, he combined both these professions simultaneously. In 1937–38 he served as a Soviet Military Adviser in Spain. He took part in air battles and shot down several enemy aircraft. At the same time he carried out a series of first-class recruitments amongst internationalists of many countries and assured a regular flow of military and military-technical intelligence. On his return from Spain he became chief of the GRU, a post he occupied from the end of 1938 to July 1940. He openly came out against the pact with Hitler. On the 4 July 1940 he was arrested, and the following day shot without trial.

Marshal of the Soviet Union GOLIKOV, Filipp Ivanovich: 16.7.1900 - 29.6.1980.
He entered the Red Army as a volunteer in 1918 and took an active part in the suppression of anti-communist peasant riots on the staff of the 3rd Army Special Punitive Brigades. After the civil war he commanded a regiment, brigade, division and corps. In September 1939 he fought in Poland as commander of the 6th Army. In 1940 he became the chief of the GRU. After Hitler's invasion and the loss of contact with the most important agent network he transferred the GRU command point from Moscow to London under the guise of the Soviet military mission. In October 1941 he returned to the USSR. He commanded an army, then a front. From April 1943 he was deputy to Stalin for Red Army cadres, and, at the same time, from 1944 directed operations against the Russian Liberation Army and the search for, and liquidation of, the leaders and those taking part in the Russian anti-communist opposition. Golikov *de facto* directed the forcible

repatriation and destruction of more than a million people who did not want to return to the USSR. Golikov directed the post-war purge of the Army. When it was over he himself was removed from all his posts. He spent two years in prison, but by 1950 he was commanding another army and, from 1956, he was Academy Chief. From 1958 he was head of the Chief Political Directorate of the Soviet Army and, simultaneously, Director of a Party Central Committee Department. Golikov agreed to be Army Controller on the side of the Party. In 1961 he was made Marshal of the Soviet Union. In May 1962 he was removed from office without much rumpus or scandal, however. Golikov may be said to have had the most distinguished career in the whole Soviet Army.

From July 1941 to July 1942 Aleksei Pavlovich PANFILOV was Chief of the GRU. He was shot in 1942. In 1942–43 the GRU leadership was held by Ivan Ivanovich ILICHEV. He was also shot.

Colonel-General KUZNETSOV, Fedor Fedotovich: 6.2.1904 - 1979.
A country boy who came to Moscow and became a factory worker, he quickly assessed the situation, joined the Party and embarked on an meteoric career. By 1937 he was 1st Secretary of the Proletarski district of Moscow, and in the heat of the great purge he showed exceptional cruelty. In 1938 he was called up into the Army and appointed deputy head of the Chief Political Directorate. He was an active participant in the army purge which included the GRU, and from 1943 he was chief of the GRU. On his appointment Stalin asked him whether he could be as good an intelligence officer as he had been earlier Party Controller of the Army. Kuznetsov's reply—'Is there any great difference?'—has become proverbial. Kuznetsov at work demonstrated that there was no great difference between the cruel, bloody struggle within the party and intelligence work. He was one of the cruellest but also one of the most successful chiefs of the GRU. In 1943 he received the plans of operation 'Citadel' (the German attack near Kursk) before General-Field Marshal E. von Manstein, whose duty it was to implement those plans. Kuznetsov had a special role to play in the organisation and carrying out of the great powers' conference in Teheran and, as a reward for his success in this, received the rank of Colonel-General. In 1945 he played an active part in the preparations and implementation of the Yalta and Potsdam conferences and also personally directed operations to steal American atomic technology.
   In 1948, at the height of the post-war purges Stalin appointed Kuznetsov supreme Party Controller of the Army – Head of the Chief Political Directorate. He held this post right up to the time of Stalin's death, mercilessly purging the Soviet Army of dissidents. After Stalin's death a slow decline set in, first to the post of Head of the Chief Personnel Directorate at the Ministry of Defence, then Academy Head and, finally, Head of the Political Directorate of the Northern Group of Forces. He retired in 1969.

General of the Army SHTEMYENKO, Sergei Matveevich: 7.2.1907 - 23.4.1976.
Shtemyenko joined the Red Army as a volunteer. He completed military training and two academy courses, and from 1940 was on the General Staff. His rise was swift. In 1943 he was head of the Operations Directorate of the General Staff and one of the principal Soviet military planners and the closest to Stalin. He accompanied Stalin to the Teheran conference. He became chief of the GRU from April 1946, General of the Army and Chief of the General Staff from November 1948. In June 1952, at the time of the squabble between Stalin and the Politburo he came out on Stalin's side and was, by Politburo decree, stripped of all his posts, demoted to Lieut-General and despatched to command the Volga military

district staff. In 1956, at Marshal Zhukov's demand, he was returned to Moscow, reinstated in his rank of General of the Army and re-appointed chief of the GRU. In October 1957 during the conspiracy against Zhukov, he came out on Zhukov's side. Once again he was stripped of his offices, demoted to Lieut-General and sent off to command a military district staff. In June 1962 he was Chief of Staff for Land Forces. In 1968 his rank of General of the Army was restored and he was appointed First Deputy Chief of the General Staff – Chief of Staff of the Warsaw Pact. He was still in favour when he died.

Shtemyenko's career was feverish as well as resilient. He was put forward three times for the rank of Marshal of the Soviet Union, the first time at the age of forty-one, but he never received the honour. He is considered to have been the most energetic, erudite and merciless of all GRU chiefs.

General of the Army KURASOV, Vladimir Vasilievich: 7.7.1897 - 29.11.73.
A Russian Army officer who went over to the side of the communists after the revolution. He served on various staffs, and from 1940 was deputy head of the General Staff Operations Directorate. During the war he was Chief of Staff of the 4th Shock Army, and later a front. After the war he was Commander-in-Chief of the Central group of forces in Austria. Promoted General of the Army, he was made chief of the GRU in February 1949. In the same year he was removed from this office and appointed Chief of the General Staff Academy. From 1956–61 he was Deputy Chief of the General Staff. His career ran smoothly. It has been said that, having accepted the GRU post and learning of the fate of all his predecessors Kurasov, on a specious pretext, declined the office and transferred to a less hazardous post. This story is corroborated by several independent sources

Marshal of the Soviet Union ZAKHAROV, Matvei Vasilievich: 5.8.1898 - 31.1.1972.
Zakharov was in Petrograd in the First World War and avoided being conscripted into the Army. He came out actively against the war, joined the Red Guard in April 1917 and stormed the Winter Palace. He then took part in the suppression of anti-communist manifestations and held unimportant posts in the Red Army. By 1936 he had worked himself up to the command of a regiment. The great purge opened up many vacancies, and in July 1937 Zakharov was Chief of Staff of the Leningrad Military District, and, from May 1938, Deputy Chief of the General Staff. During the war he was Chief of Staff of the 9th Army and later front, and, after the war, Head of the General Staff Academy. He became chief of the GRU in January 1949. In June 1952 a fierce struggle broke out about convening the 19th Party Congress. The Politburo insisted, Stalin objected. The Chief of the General Staff Shtemyenko, and the Chief of the GRU Zakharov, supported Stalin and were dismissed from their posts. After Stalin's death Zakharov's fall continued, but in May 1953 he was appointed Commander of the Leningrad Military District and was able to hold on to this post. In October 1957 a struggle broke out between the Politburo and Marshal Zhukov. Zakharov was fully on the side of the Politburo and for this he was immediately appointed Commander-in-Chief of the Group of Soviet Forces in Germany. In 1959 he was made Marshal of the Soviet Union, and Chief of the General Staff in 1960. In 1963 he was dismissed. He took an active part in the conspiracy against Khruschev and, after the successful *coup d'état* was re-appointed Chief of the General Staff where he served up to September 1971—practically up to the time of his death.

Colonel-General SHALIN, Mikhail Alekseevich was chief of the GRU from 1951-56 and from November 1957 to December 1958.

General of the Army SEROV, Ivan Alekseevich.
An officer of military intelligence, at the time of the purges of the GRU he managed not only to survive but also to transfer to work in the NKVD. On 12 June 1937 he appeared in the capacity of executioner of Marshal Tukhachevski and other leading figures of the Red Army. Amongst all the protagonists of the terror he distinguished himself as the most fervent exponent of 'scenes on a massive scale'. He took part in the pursuit and liquidation of the inhabitants of Estonia, Latvia and Lithuania in 1940 and in 1944–47. Data exists as to his personal involvement in the murder of the Polish officers in Katyn. During the war Serov was one of the leaders of Smersh, and in August 1946 he personally took part in the execution of the command of the Russian Liberation Army under Lieut-General Vlasov. Subsequently he betrayed his leaders in Smersh and the NKGB, going over in time to the camp of the victorious groups. He deserted Abakumov's group for that of Beria and betrayed him (as did General Ivashutin – the present GRU leader). In 1953 he was deputy chief of the GRU and one of the conspirators against Beria. After the fall of Beria, Serov became Chairman of the KGB. Together with Ambassador Andropov he seized the leaders of the Hungarian revolution by deceit and took part in their torture and execution. In December 1958 Serov became chief of the GRU. As an ex-KGB and Smersh officer he had many enemies in the GRU. Under Serov's leadership, corruption in GRU attained unbelievable proportions. In 1962 he was dismissed and quietly liquidated.

Serov's was the dirtiest career in the history of the GRU. He displayed a high degree of personal sadism. The years when Serov was chief of the GRU were also the most unproductive in its history. It was the only period when GRU officers voluntarily made contact with Western services and gave them much more valuable information than they took from them.

General of the Army IVASHUTIN, Peter Ivanovitch: 5.9.1909 -
A volunteer in the punitive formations of the Special Purpose Units, Ivashutin came into Army counter-intelligence from 1931. During the war he held leading posts in Smersh. Even at this time Ivashutin had powerful enemies in the NKGB. In 1944–45 he was chief of Smersh on the 3rd Ukrainian Front and in that capacity waged a ferocious struggle against the Ukrainian insurgent army and played an active role in the establishment of communist order in Bulgaria, Yugoslavia and Hungary. It was at this time that he first met Brezhnev, and in all subsequent activities the two men always supported each other. At the end of the war Ivashutin took part in the forcible repatriation of Soviet citizens who did not want to return to the Soviet Union. He also played a special part in the liquidation of soldiers and officers of the Russian Liberation Army. After the disbandment of Smersh he managed to outlive its other leaders by a timely transfer out of the Abakumov faction into that of Beria. At Beria's downfall he went over to the Serov faction and was appointed head of the KGB 3rd Chief Directorate. He then took part in the arrest and liquidation of Serov. On Brezhnev's recommendation in 1963, Ivashutin was appointed chief of the GRU. In this position he had a number of very serious confrontations with the KGB and personally with Andropov. However, Ivashutin defended the interests of the Army with more vigour than any of his predecessors and, therefore, in spite of his past ties with the KGB, enjoyed unlimited support from the first deputy chairman of the Council of Ministers, the chairman of the Military Industrial Complex Smirnov as well as Marshals Ustinov and Ogarkov. After Andropov's coming to power Ivashutin held on to his post in view of powerful support within the Army.

Appendix B

The GRU High Command and Leading GRU Officers

The following list gives names of the most prominent senior GRU officers with their official titles where possible. This is followed by an alphabetical list of some of the known operational officers working under cover around the world.

Army General IVASHUTIN, Petr Ivanovich: deputy chief of the General Staff of the Soviet Armed Forces. Head of GRU. Official pseudonyms 'Tovarishch Mikhailov', 'Dyadya Petya'. The first pseudonym is also used in connection with all military intelligence.
Col-General LEMZENKO, Kir Gavirlovich: GRU representative in the Party Central Committee; 'Papa Rimski'.
Col-General PAVLOV, Aleksandr Grigorevich: first deputy chief of GRU.
Admiral BEKRENEV: deputy chief of GRU.
Col-General ZOTOV, Arkady Vasilievich: deputy chief of GRU, head of Information.
Col-General MESHCHERYAKOV, V.V.: deputy chief of GRU, head of the Military Diplomatic Academy.
Col-General IZOTOV, S.I.: head of GRU Personnel Directorate.
Col-General SIDOROV, Y.I.

Lieutenant-Generals and Vice Admirals (approximately 20)
Lt-General DOLIN, G.I.: head of GRU Political Department.
Lt-General GURENKO, Vyacheslav Tikhonovich: head of the Illegals Training Centre.
Lt-General Aviation SHATALOV, Vladimir Aleksandrovich: GRU representative at the Cosmonaut Training Centre.
Lt-General KOLODYAZHNY, Boris Gavrilovich: GRU deputy chief for Internal Security.
Lt-General MILSTEIN, Moshe: GRU deputy chief for Disinformation. A former illegal and author of top secret manual *Honourable Service*. Codename 'Tovarishch M', 'Mikhail M.'.
Lt-General KOSTIN P.T.: chief of GRU 3rd (?) Directorate.
Lt-General Engineer PALIY A.: chief of GRU 6th Directorate.
Lt-General GONTAR: chief of GRU 7th Directorate.
Lt-General DRACHEV I.M.
Lt-General KOZLOV M.: Chief of GRU 11th (?) Directorate.
Lt-General BERKUTOV, S.: Information Service.
Vice Admiral ROZHKO, Gennadi Aleksandrovich.

Major-Generals and Rear Admirals (approximately 125)
Maj-General Aviation CHIZHOV, Mikhail Terentyevich.
Rear Admiral KALININ, Valeri Petrovich.
Maj-General Aviation KUCHUMOV, Aleksandr Mikhailovich.
Maj-General SHITOV.
Rear Admiral KLYUZOV, Serafim Timofeevich.
Maj-General BARANOV, Aleksandr Vasilievich.
Maj-General LYALIN, Mikhail Ammosovich.
Maj-General BEPPAEV S.U.: Chief of Intelligence of Group Soviet Forces in Germany.
Maj-General Artillery LYUBIMOV, Viktor Andreevich.
Maj-General GONCHAROV, Gennadi Grigorevich.
Maj-General KHOMYAKOV, Aleksandr Sergeevich.
Rear Admiral KOZLOV, Andrei Nikolaevich.
Maj-General MIKHAILOV, Boris Nikolaevich.
Maj-General ZIMIN, Valentin Yakovlevich.
Maj-General ANDRYANOV, V.: *Spetsnaz.*
Maj-General Aviation MIKRYUKOV, L.
Maj-General GLAZUNOV, N.
Rear Admiral SMIRNOV, M.

Leading GRU Officers
ABRAMOV, Vladimir Mikhailovich
BAYLIN, Vladimir Ivanovich
BELOUSOV, Mikolai Mikhailovich
BELOUSOV, Konstantin Nikolaevich
BLINOV, Boris Afanasyevich
BARCHUGOV
BORISOV, Gennadi Alekseevich
BORODIN, Viktor Mikhailovich
BUDENNY
BOROVINSKI, Petr Fedorovich
BUBNOV, Nikolai Ivanovich
BUTAKOV, Ilya Petrovich
DEMIN, Mikhail Alekseevich
DENISOV
DORONKIN, Kirill Sergeevich
EGOROV, Anatoli Egorovich
ERMAKOV, Aleksandr Ivanovich
ERSHOV, Yuri Alekseevich
EVDOKIMOV, Sergei Vasilevich
FEKLENKO, Vladimir Nikolaevich
FILATOV, Anatoli
FILIPPOV, Anatoli Vasilevich
GENERALOV, Vsevolod Nikolaevich
GERASIMOV
KAPALKIN, Sergei Vasilevich
KASHEVAROV, Evgeni Mikhailovich
KOZYPITSKI, Gleb Sergeevich
LOVCHIKOV, Vasili Dmitrievich
LAVROV, Valeri Alecseevich

183

LEMEKHOV, Dmitri Aleksandrovich
LOBANOV, Vitali Ilich
LOGINOV, Igor Konstantinovich
MOROZOV, Ivan Yakovlevich
MYAKISHEV, Aleksei Nikolaevich
NEDOZOROV, Valentin Viktorovich
NOSKOV, Nikolai Stepanovich
OSIPOV, Oleg Aleksandrovich
PAVLENKO, Yuri Kuzmich
PETROV, Nikolai Kirillovich
PIVOBAROV, Oleg Ivanovich
POLYAKOV, Boris Alekseevich
POPOV, Gennadi Fedorovich
POTAPENKO, Leonid Terentyevich
POTSELUEV, Evgeni Aleksandrovich
PUTILIN, Mikhail Semenovich
RATNIKOV, Valentin Mikhailovich
RADIONOV, Aleksandr Sergeevich
ROMANOV, Anatoli Aleksandrovich
RUBANOV, Aleksandr Nikolaevich
SALEKHOV, Yuri Nikolaevich
SAVIN, Viktor Grigorevich
SELUNSKI, Valentin Ivanovich
SEMENOV, Aleksandr Aleksandrovich
SERGEEV, Yuri Pavlovich
SHEPELEV, Viktor Petrovich
SHIPOV, Vladilen Nikolaevich
SOKOLOV, Viktor Aleksandrovich
STRELBITSKI, Vladimir Vasilevich
STUDENIKIN, Ivan Yakovlevich
SUKHAREV, Georgi Nikolaevich
SUVOROV, Georgi Borisovich
UMNOV, Valentin Aleksandrovich
VETROV, Yuri Pavlovich
VILKOV, Boris Nikolaevich
VINOGRADOV, Feliks Vasilevich
VOLNOV, Vladimir Grigorevich
VOLOKITIN, Vladimir Ivanovich
VOTRIN, Sergei Ivanovich
VYBORNOV, Ivan Yakovlevich
YAKUSHEV, Ivan Ivanovich
YURASOV, Viktor Vladimirovich
ZHELANNOV, Vladimir Mikhailovich
ZHEREBTSON, Aleksandr Vasilevich
ZHERNOV, Leonid Andreevich
ZHURAVLEV, Ivan Mikhailovich
ZOTOV, Viktor Nikolaevich

Appendix C

Some Case Histories of GRU Activities

Rather than sprinkling the text with examples I have put together a representative sample of GRU officers uncovered in the course of operations abroad, as reported in the press. The number of GRU officers caught and expelled and the nature of their activities is indicative of the power and scale of the GRU.

Canada and the United States
In June 1980 the Canadians announced that they had requested the withdrawal of three Soviet officials from the Embassy, Captain Igor A. Bardeev, Colonel E.I. Aleksanjan and the chauffeur Sokolov. The case involved an unnamed individual employed in a sensitive position in the USA, who had been in contact with the Soviet Embassy and been given the task of obtaining information. Soviet officials had maintained clandestine contact with the American citizen over a period of some months.

France
In October 1979 the Naval and Air Attaché of the Soviet Embassy in France, Vladimïr Kulik, was expelled from the country. He was an officer of the GRU working in French military circles and had been in contact with firms specialising in military supplies. In 1979, at a reception in another embassy, he had met by chance a young Frenchman employed in the armaments department of an important organisation who was carrying out studies on behalf of the Ministry of Defence. Kulik sought to maintain contact with the Frenchman, and in due course offered him a large sum of money for documents from his place of work. He also sought to find out details about other staff at the organisation where the Frenchman worked. Kulik was arrested at the moment when he was about to receive from the Frenchman a document about a French weapon.

In February 1980 the Soviet Consul and No. 2 in Marseilles was withdrawn. He had been detained by the French authorities between Toulon and Marseilles with plans of the Mirage 2000 fighter aircraft in his briefcase. They had just been handed to him by an agent.

Travkov had arrived in 1977. The area of Marseilles and the Bouches du Rhône contains many installations and objects of defence interest. Travkov was officially concerned with 'scientific subjects connected with the port and airport', and these interests enabled him to meet people involved in the aeronautical field and to visit firms and installations. Travkov obtained copies of files on staff working on defence contracts and used the details thus revealed to build up a network of informers. Four Frenchmen were taken into custody at the time of Travkov's arrest. Travkov had also been interested in the twin-jet Mirage 4000 which used the same engine as the 2000.

The Soviet Press Attaché declared the French action a 'provocation by the police' but the documents were, of course, genuine. A few days later Frolov, himself a KGB officer, was required to leave France too. He had been in Marseilles for two years and had earlier had a posting to Paris. His job, like Travkov's, had given him opportunities to meet all sorts of people and he had made the most of it. Both Travkov and Frolov were personable, charming individuals who made many friends.

Great Britain
Anatoliy Pavlovich Zotov, the Soviet Naval Attaché in London, was expelled in December 1982 after trying to set up a network of agents to gather information about weapons systems and electronic hardware used by the Royal Navy during the Falklands campaign. His interests had also extended to the Royal Navy's nuclear submarines.

Japan
A retired Japanese major-general, Yukihisa Miyanaga was arrested in Tokyo in January 1980. He was a GRU agent whose case officer at the time of his arrest was Colonel Yuriy N. Koslov, Military and Air Attaché at the Soviet Embassy. Miyanaga had been recruited as an agent in 1974 by one of Koslov's predecessors. He was equipped with and instructed in various means of clandestine communication, including particular ciphers for use with radio. Miyanaga and two other officers of the Japanese Ground Self-Defence Force were subsequently sentenced to long terms of imprisonment for passing military secrets to the GRU.

Norway
Valeriy Moiseevich Mesropov served in Norway as an engineer with a Russian firm in Drammen, as a representative of Stankoimport, from 1968 to 1970. Mesropov, who was not a diplomat, was arrested in 1970 on suspicion of intelligence activity and finally expelled from Norway for security reasons in September 1970.

Igor Ivanovich Zashchirinsky served in Norway from 1974 to 1977 as representative at the Soviet Trade Delegation of a number of Soviet import/export organisations. He was engaged on clandestine operations to obtain information and products of a scientific/technical nature including material classified as Top Secret. He too was declared *persona non grata* on 28 January 1977.

In June 1983 Lt-Colonel Zagrebnev was expelled from Norway. He was Military Attaché at the Embassy in Oslo, and had visited a military area in the north of Norway, where he had attempted to bribe a Norwegian officer to hand over secret information.

Spain
Oleg Churanov, Director of Aeroflot in Madrid, was arrested in February 1980, accused of espionage for the Soviet Union. His case was part of another expulsion of six officials who had already left. It was alleged that Churanov had bought plans of certain aviation electronic equipment. The 'seller' was a member of the Spanish Secret Services who purported to be a member of a Spanish firm. Churanov was an engineer who had been Aeroflot representative in Canada before coming to Spain. He was very popular with staff and pilots at Madrid airport where he had shown interest in radio frequencies and the security

regulations at the airport. He had also tried, on one occasion, to get a Spanish pilot to introduce him into the American airport at Tarrejon. The Spanish security authorities themselves claimed that Churanov was a member of the GRU.

In May 1982 the Aeroflot Director in Spain was again expelled for spying, this time with another official. Vasiliy Fedorin and Vladimir Tertishnikov were accused of trying to obtain information on the supply of US military materials to Spain and on Spanish weapons manufacturers.

Sweden
In March 1979 Stig Bergling, a Swedish police inspector and reserve officer, was arrested in Israel. He had been an agent of the GRU for some ten years. In January 1969 he had begun service with the Police Board, and from 1971–75 was given leave of absence to serve in the Defence Ministry and to do duty with the UN.

Bergling had access to information about security police personnel and counter-espionage organisations; and about defence establishments and Swedish defence plans. He was equipped with radio to receive messages from the GRU, and also made use of micro-dots. He kept in touch with his case officers in a number of countries, particularly in the Middle East, having been trained in East Berlin.

Index